PEACE
in Our Hearts,

PEACE
in the World

PEACE

in Our Hearts,

PEACE

in the World

MEDITATIONS OF HOPE AND HEALING

Ruth Fishel

12-8-11
With Love
~
Peace-
Ruth

STERLING

New York / London
www.sterlingpublishing.com

STERLING and the distinctive Sterling logo are
registered trademarks of Sterling Publishing Co., Inc.

Library of Congress Cataloging-in-Publication Data

Fishel, Ruth, 1935-
    Peace in our hearts, peace in the world : meditations of hope and healing / Ruth Fishel.
        p. cm.
    Includes bibliographical references and index.
    ISBN 978-1-4027-5717-4 (alk. paper)
    1. Meditations. 2. Devotional calendars. 3. Peace--Religious aspects--Meditations. I. Title.
    BL624.2.F57 2008
    158.1'28--dc22

                                    2008024991

10   9   8   7   6   5   4   3   2   1

Published by Sterling Publishing Co., Inc.
387 Park Avenue South, New York, NY 10016
© 2008 by Ruth Fishel
Distributed in Canada by Sterling Publishing
C/o Canadian Manda Group, 165 Dufferin Street
Toronto, Ontario, Canada M6K 3H6
Distributed in the United Kingdom by GMC Distribution Services
Castle Place, 166 High Street, Lewes, East Sussex, England BN7 1XU
Distributed in Australia by Capricorn Link (Australia) Pty. Ltd.
P.O. Box 704, Windsor, NSW 2756, Australia

Book design and layout: Christine Kwasnik

Manufactured in the United States of America
All rights reserved

Sterling ISBN 978-1-4027-5717-4

For information about custom editions, special sales, premium
and corporate purchases, please contact Sterling Special Sales
Department at 800-805-5489 or specialsales@sterlingpublishing.com.

With deep gratitude I dedicate this book to my readers
who are sending the energy of peace
into the hearts and lives of all beings everywhere.

If there is to be peace in the world,
There must be peace in the nations.
If there is to be peace in the nations,
There must be peace in the cities.
If there is to be peace in the cities,
There must be peace between neighbors.
If there is to be peace between neighbors,
There must be peace in the home.
If there is to be peace in the home,
There must be peace in the heart.
—Lao-tzu

Dear Friends,

We may be in the most peaceful place in the world, but if we do not have inner peace, we will not feel peaceful. And yet we may find ourselves in the midst of turmoil and strife, and if we do have inner peace, then we *can* feel peaceful.

It all begins with us. By taking just a few quiet minutes each day and meditating on peace, we can become peaceful. And once we are peaceful, that feeling will expand out into the universe, touching those around us.

The words that we speak, read, and think are very powerful! *Peace in Our Hearts, Peace in the World* is filled with powerful, stimulating, inspirational words. Imagine many thousands of people reading the same page, the same message, each day and the lasting effect that it would have on each of them as well as on the people with whom they come in contact.

When enough people join in taking just a few moments a day to meditate for peace, in time there will be peace in this world . . . forever. We actually do have the power to make that happen. This might sound like a grandiose, overenthusiastic, exaggerated claim, but I truly believe that I was inspired to write this book and I am deeply grateful and humbled to share it with you.

Each page in *Peace in Our Hearts, Peace in the World* represents one day. Spend a few minutes each day being with the thoughts on just one page.

Think about them. Sit quietly with them. Meditate on them.

Let the feelings of the words fill you with peace and strength and then carry that feeling with you for the rest of your day, sharing it with others as you move through the hours.

As you read these daily pages, watch your life change. Know that you are connected with countless like-minded people reading the same page each day and feel how powerful this is.

Know that you can make at least one positive change in your life, and thus affect the lives of those around you, each day. It does not have to be big or great. Just one thing to make your life more peaceful. Just one thing. One small thing.

Know that you can make a difference.

Know that you do make a difference.

Know that you are making a difference.

Thank you for joining me and all the others who are passing on the power of thought, prayer, and meditation so that the horrors of war can cease and there can be peace for all human beings!

It is time for Peace in Our Hearts, Peace in the World.

With love, peace, and gratitude,

—Ruth Fishel
Cape Cod
September 2007

WITH DEEP GRATITUDE

I am deeply grateful to:

Sandy Bierig, for her tireless editing and support.

My agent Nigel J. Yorwerth, for his belief in this book, and Patricia Spadaro, for her help with the proposal.

The people at Sterling Publishing Co., Inc., who had faith in me and who could see the importance of this book, and David Nelson, Kate Zimmermann, Anne Barthel, and Hannah Reich, for their insights and clarity.

To the following people who have contributed such wonderful pages: Dorna L. Allen, Deb Bergstrom, Sandy Bierig, Debbie Boisseau, Tommie Ann Bower, Jo Chaffee, Michael Collins, Rev. Steve Carty Cordry, David A. Cronin, Diane Crosby, James F. David, M. Div., Rev. Marie David, Jane Drury, Jeff Eagle, Nancy Jo Ericson, Judy Fishel, Janet Glass, Joanne Friday, Debbie Hagen, Rachel Hamel, Meredith Jordan, James W. Kershner, Kathy Kidd, Tom E. Largy, Mary Jane LaVigne, Heather Lowe, Sandy Martin, Gail McMeekin, Joy Miller, PhD, Delle Moore, Gina Ogden, PhD, Sister Kay O'Neil, PBVM, Hannah Reich, Steffi L. Shapiro, Amy Shore, Patricia Spadaro, Barbara Thomas, Kelly Warren, Samantha White, and Nigel J. Yorwerth.

To those who read the early drafts, who searched for typos, and had such wonderful suggestions: Jane Drury, Constance Sable, Diana Smith, and Barbara Thomas.

To all my teachers: Sylvia Boorstein, Christina Feldman, Joanne Friday, Joseph Goldstein, Jack Kornfield, Narayan Liebenson Grady, Joanne Friday, Thich Nhat Hanh, Jim Kershner, Larry Rosenberg, Sharon Salzberg; and my special friends; authors; and workshops leaders who have taught me so much over the years.

To Dr. Bob and Bill Wilson. Without them I would not be here today.

> Deep peace of the running wave to you.
> Deep peace of the flowing air to you.
> Deep peace of the quiet earth to you.
> Deep peace of the shining stars to you.
> —Celtic blessing

Peace is everywhere. Peace is in the waves and the flowing air, the quiet earth and the shining stars. Peace is in church and in temple and in the mosque and the synagogue. Peace is in the forest and the hills and the desert.

But when we are full of fear or anger, frustration or stress, how can we find it? How can we achieve this deep peace when life isn't going our way, when a loved one dies or our business fails, when our spouse wants a divorce or our child is caught in drug addiction?

How can we feel this peace that poets and mystics talk and write about so eloquently and invitingly? And how can we possibly pass it on to others? No matter what is going on in the outside world, we can look deep into our own hearts. Peace is always there. This precious, mysterious, mystical God-given gift lies within us always waiting to be found. It is as close as this moment, this instant, this breath. Peace is right here for us to feel and nurture and share with the rest of the world.

I am so grateful to know that no matter what is going on in my life today, I can always find peace in my heart. And once found, it is my privilege and joy to share it with others.

> *Greater in combat than the person who conquers a thousand*
> *times a thousand people is the person who conquers himself.*
> —The Buddha

If we can't stop the battles in our minds, how can we expect to stop the battles in the world? We need to begin with ourselves and first understand our own personal conflicts.

Are we at war with our food, our weight, drugs, or alcohol? Do we spend more than we can afford? Are we going back and forth between *should I* and *shouldn't I*? Do we struggle with fear versus faith, selfishness versus generosity, and so forth? It is helpful to observe whatever it is with which we struggle. This is no different from the struggle between two people, two families, two communities, or two nations. As we become willing to resolve our own inner struggles, outside issues often resolve themselves. Each time we are willing to look at our own issues, we come to a greater understanding of the conflicts others face.

We can begin to learn to stop our own wars before
attempting to stop the wars of the world.
Today I am willing to watch my own inner battlefield
with compassion, praying for the understanding and
resolution of the conflict so I can find peace.

Today
I
will
move
from
my
head
to
my
heart
and
choose
LOVE
and
PEACE.

*If you are the recipient, giver, or observer of an act
of kindness, your serotonin levels are increased and
your immune system is strengthened.*

—Wayne Dyer

Sometimes we can be filled with a most incredible feeling of joy simply by witnessing an act of kindness. We don't need to be involved except with our eyes and our hearts to feel an indescribable fullness, which may be accompanied by lumps in our throats or tears in our eyes. I experienced all of this one day when my car was stopped behind a school bus. A small child stepped off the bus and ran into the arms of her grinning father.

Once, when I was going through a particularly painful time after my son died unexpectedly, my son-in-law presented me with a birdhouse he had built himself and painted purple, my very favorite color. My daughter-in-law gave me a ceramic fox, symbolic of my son's favorite animal. On both occasions, instant tears surprised me as my heart swelled with love and gratitude.

Watch someone's face as you surprise him or her with an unexpected gift or compliment. No matter what mood you might be in at the time, you will be filled with joy or love or gratitude, with a flow of feel-good chemicals spreading throughout your body and mind.

*It feels so good to know that when I do something kind,
I am not only feeling good and helping someone else feel good,
but strengthening my immune system at the same time.
Today I am taking the time to do something kind for someone.*

My mind is a garden. My thoughts are the seeds.
My harvest will be either flower or weeds.
—Mel Weldon

Our thoughts create our feelings. When we truly understand the implications of this, we can experience tremendous freedom. No longer do we need to be victims of other people or of our past. We see that we can be responsible for our lives! We can choose to think thoughts that create happiness, love, and compassion rather than anger, fear, or bitterness.

As we grow in our ability to be mindful of how we speak to ourselves, we discover whether we are being judges, critics, friends, or cheerleaders. This takes practice, and it is important to remember that we are moving toward progress, not perfection. At first, the voice of our inner judge or critic might be the loudest we hear because it has been in charge for so many years. Once we get in touch with this tendency, we can choose to let that voice evaporate and replace it with words from our inner friend or cheerleader.

It feels so good to practice speaking to myself
with love and compassion today. I no longer need
the judge and the critic in my life.

*Solitude—walking alone, doing things alone—
is the most blessed thing in the world. The mind relaxes
and thoughts begin to flow and I think I am beginning
to find myself a little bit.*

—Helen Hayes

It is good to take time each day to get away from the turmoil of our daily routines and rest in solitude. It helps us to renew, to connect with our inner resources, and to find serenity. Solitude can be a time for inner reflection, a time to become centered and to find our connection with God. Solitude can lift our spirits in times of need. We can discover where we belong in the universe and find our own true purpose. In solitude we can reach a place deep inside ourselves where we can find peace.

In quiet times we can listen to what is real in our hearts and become more and more familiar with ourselves. We can truly come to know ourselves, all of ourselves, for the beautiful people that we are.

*Today I am taking time alone to find inner peace, to get
to know myself better, and to see that I am becoming
the beautiful person God intended me to be.*

> Mindfulness is the miracle by which we can
> master and restore ourselves . . . Whenever your mind
> becomes scattered, use your breath as the means to take
> hold of your mind again.
>
> —Thich Nhat Hanh

This is a very short and simple lesson in mindfulness, a way in which we can bring peace to ourselves in any moment. Practicing this twenty minutes each day, preferably in the morning, will change your life.

Sit comfortably, with your back as straight as possible. Let your entire body relax. Close your eyes very gently. Bring your full awareness to your breath as you breathe in and out through your nose. You can say to yourself: "I am breathing in. I am breathing out. In. Out." Or: "I am breathing in peace. I am breathing out tension. Peace. Tension."

Simply notice whatever takes you away from your breathing—a thought, sound, itch, daydream—and acknowledge it by naming it. Then, very gently, without judgment, go back to your breathing.

By practicing this twenty minutes in the morning, every day, you will learn how powerful your breath is, and you will become more and more aware that you can turn to your breath at any time during the day to bring peace to your heart.

> Today I am giving myself the gift of mindfulness.
> I am practicing sitting with my breath for at least twenty
> minutes and feeling the joy of serenity and peace.
> I am carrying this peace with me for the rest of the day.

We
can't
have
peace
in
the
world
until
we
have
peace
in
our
hearts.

> To accept ourselves as we are means to value our
> imperfections as much as our perfections.
> —Sandy Bierig

When we simply accept what is, neither good nor bad, right nor wrong, we sit in the pure space of now, in this one moment in time.

When we see ourselves, all of ourselves, just as we are, without judgments, without looking at ourselves as we think others see us, we can find peace. If we can do this, we have a much better chance of accepting others just as they are. Our relationships with other people improve. Our own self-esteem improves.

Acceptance leads to peace and feels so good.
Today I am being very gentle with myself and
accepting myself just as I am.

Light tomorrow with today.
—Elizabeth Barrett Browning

Today I am learning that I have a choice in each moment. What I choose to do with this moment affects my future. When I am aware of that, I can act in ways that will bring happiness and satisfaction to my todays and tomorrows. When I forget that, I am at the whim of anything and anyone that comes my way. I feel so much more peaceful when I keep this knowledge in the forefront of my mind. I can feel all my tension melting away and being replaced with positive energy. It feels so good to know that I am doing what I can to create a positive, peaceful future.

I am mindful of what I am doing and thinking today,
knowing that each moment affects the next moment;
each day affects the next day.

There is a purpose for our existence which, at times,
transcends human understanding.
—Aphrodite Matsakis

Some of us, a rare few, discover our purpose early in our childhood. The child prodigy who plays the piano at the age of two, for example, or the girl who knows by the time she is five that she wants to be a doctor and actually goes on to become one. For most of us, our purpose takes much longer to discover and often comes with trial and error and great struggle.

Some of us never do have a clear idea of a purpose, of a profession or talent that is right for us. But we find we are doing God's will in many ways. Practicing being a good parent, a kind and compassionate person, or a generous benefactor can fill us with a sense of purpose.

As long as we continue to grow along a spiritual path, we find ways to be useful and bring meaning to our lives, lifting our own spirits and the spirits of those around us. Living a life of purpose fills us with inner peace and joy.

Today I pray for the knowledge of God's will
for me and the power to carry it out.

> *Listening to the silence immediately*
> *creates stillness inside you.*
>
> —Eckhart Tolle

Stop.
Listen to the silence.
Take a moment to be aware of your breath as you
        breathe in and
        breathe out.
Be still.
Listen to the silence.

Be aware of the silence with every God-filled breath. Feel your chest rising and falling, your stomach filling and emptying. Nothing more. Nothing less. Stay with the silence. No televisions or radios. No phones. Nothing. Take some time each day to listen to the silence.

Feel the depth of the silence.
Feel the peace in the silence.

> *Today, as I take time to be quiet, to listen to the silence,*
> *I find deep peace. I can return to this place wherever I am,*
> *in a crowd or alone, releasing stress and tension, connecting*
> *with God, just by following my breath.*

*The expression of praise as gratitude and joy is among
the most powerful forms of affirmation.*
—Catherine Ponder

For so many years I craved being praised and appreciated. When it came to me, I felt so good—but just for a while. Then the warm feelings faded and I hungered for the next compliment, the next sign that I was worth something.

Now, for the most part, I find my self-worth in who I am. No matter what mood I am in, my spirits lift when I remember to find something for which to be grateful. And how wonderful to discover that when I praise someone else, the action fills my spirit as well as theirs. The added blessing is that by expressing my appreciation to another person, I am sending out positive energy into the world and living in it as well.

*I am filled with joy and peace as I express my
appreciation to others whenever possible.*

We are what we repeatedly do.

—*Aristotle*

Take some time today to be mindful of your thoughts. Don't judge them as right or wrong. Simply notice them with gentleness. As you notice them, follow that observation to the next step by watching how you feel with each thought. And then follow what you do with your feelings.

Our actions come from our thoughts. By being aware of which thought triggered which feeling and in turn triggered which behavior, we can be in charge of our actions. We can create new habits and become the people we choose to be.

We can come from a place of peace and love.

Today I am watching my thoughts. My intention is to create new habits, making sure my actions result from peaceful and loving thoughts. It feels so good to know that when I feel more peaceful, I am sending energy of peace out into the world with my actions.

When the soul wishes to express something,
she throws an image of the experience out before
her and enters into her own image.
—Meister Eckhart

What does peace look like for you?

Can you picture it?

Know that your soul craves peace.

Close your eyes and imagine what it would feel like if your world were peaceful.

Let your face soften and then smile as you picture a peaceful world.

Let your entire body relax, from the top of your head down to the bottom of your feet.

Breathe in peace.

Breathe out stress.

Feel the peace.

It is a beautiful feeling to know that I can
create inner peace simply by imagining it.
I am making this a regular part of my day.

*You are here to enable the divine purpose of the universe
to unfold. That is how important you are!*
—Eckhart Tolle

Living lightly is only one breath away. With willingness, the power of our intentions, combined with prayer, meditation, and positive action, we can enjoy a life of peace and purpose.

As we mature, our purpose changes. When we are young, our purpose might be to earn an education and to grow mentally, socially, and spiritually. For some of us, our purpose might be just to survive. These goals might last for many years. As we grow older, our purpose may include becoming good parents or good citizens or being financially responsible. Perhaps later the care of our own parents may be added to the list.

If we are willing to discover and let go of our blocks to peace, our hearts will continually become more and more open. We will intuitively know our next step.

*I feel blessed just knowing that God is
guiding me toward my higher purpose.*

TODAY'S PEACEFUL EXERCISE

Today I am bringing my full awareness to a daily routine.

I am being mindful of every aspect of taking a shower or a bath.

I am aware of the touch of the water and how it feels on my body.

I am aware of the smell of the soap and how it feels when I lather my body.

I am aware of the taste of the soap if I get it in my mouth when I wash my face.

I am aware of the sound of the water as it pours from the faucet.

I am aware of the sight of the water and the soap.

If thoughts take me away from my awareness, I simply notice them and return my attention to this routine.

This quiets my mind and gives me great peace.

I am carrying this peace with me for the rest of the day.

*Inner hunger is divine discontent
that keeps us moving forward.*
—Jacquelyn Small

Imagine what the world would be like if everyone were complacent and satisfied with his or her life. There would be no more improvements. Crime, abuse, war, poverty, and disease would continue unabated.

Fortunately, God has given us the drive to move forward, to create, to strive, to improve our conditions, to discover new places to explore. God doesn't let us stay complacent. When we see something that isn't right, we want to fix it.

Sometimes this desire is buried deep under fear, self-pity, or lack of self-worth or confidence, and it might take time with a therapist or spiritual advisor to uncover it. It's worth whatever it takes to clear the blocks that keep us from moving forward, and it's essential if we are to find meaning in our lives. Discovering a purpose greater than ourselves gives us the gift of inner satisfaction and peace.

God is helping me discover how to clear out the blocks that are keeping me stuck in complacency. It is exciting to know I can move forward and be a contributing member of society.

I honor
and
accept
exactly
who I am today.
I can be of use to no one else
until I accomplish this
first
for
myself.

Beginning today, treat everyone you meet as if they will not be here tomorrow. Extend to them all the care, kindness, and understanding you can muster, and do it with no thought of any reward. Your life will never be the same again.
—Og Mandino

It's easy to give love to the person we love, to be kind to the person who is kind, and to understand the person who offers us understanding. But to act with kindness and understanding to the cranky, the pushy, the mean, the selfish, and the rude—ah, that is not so easy! We most often react and want to give back what we are given, which leads us to have any feelings but peace.

No matter whom you see today, do your best to treat everyone with kindness and understanding. It might take a while to develop this habit. It might even take a lifetime. Simply making an effort is the beginning of living a more peaceful life.

Today I do not have to be an emotional victim of other people's actions. I choose to feel peace by passing on peace.

Is there
something
I can
do
for
someone
today?

Now there is silence. Seek no further.
—A Course in Miracles

No matter what is happening in our lives, we can bring our awareness to our breath and feel peace. Feeling our breath going in and going out, our chest rising and falling, our stomach filling and emptying, slows us down and brings us into the now, the present moment where peace lives.

Try it now. Breathe in and breathe out. Can you feel it? Know that whatever is going on in your life, this gift awaits you in each moment. The more you practice it, the more you will remember to use it in times of stress and anxiety.

Today I am taking time to bring my awareness to my breath,
choosing to find peace in each moment.

*Keeping hearts happy is a lot like keeping bodies healthy.
We need to feed our hearts well through reading, prayer,
and meditation, and exercise them by loving.*
—Jan Nakken

Ideas trigger thoughts. Thoughts trigger feelings. As we go through our day, it is easy to forget this, so we react to what is happening, often causing ourselves unnecessary suffering. When we do remember that thoughts are just thoughts and feelings are just feelings generated by our thoughts, we'll feel a great deal better. Reading inspirational and spiritual literature in the morning helps us because it encourages positive and loving thoughts throughout the day and keeps us connected to God.

As we meditate on the words we have read, our hearts are storing the words and the feelings they evoke. They are with us, whether we are aware of them or not. At any time during the day, we can trigger them by an act or thought of love, compassion, or generosity.

*Each morning I connect with God by taking the time,to read,
meditate, and pray. During the day I am open to God's guidance,
finding opportunities to practice being a loving person.*

Whenever you sense a feeling that is not harmonious, peaceful, and loving—all of which are your nature—you know you are out of alignment. So pause for a moment. Recognize this is not who you are or who you want to be. Take a deep breath and stop. You always have the power to pause at any moment.
—Mary Manin Morrissey

We can't always be peaceful and loving, even when we have the best intentions. Unexpected events can stimulate fear. Buttons can be pushed. A burst of anger can lead to words we later regret. No emotion is right or wrong. All emotions are natural.

It is so important that we be gentle with ourselves and accept our emotions without judgment, no matter what is going on. Acceptance releases negative energy.

Just knowing that there are times when we are powerless over our feelings can be the beginning of peace. Turning our emotions over to a power greater than ourselves, and trusting that God can and will do for us what we cannot do for ourselves, can bring us peace.

It is so comforting to know that I can turn to God and find peace, no matter what is going on in my life.

A Shinto Prayer for Peace

Although the people living across the ocean surrounding us, I believe, are all our brothers and sisters, why are there constant troubles in this world? Why do winds and waves rise in the ocean surrounding us? I only earnestly wish that the wind will soon puff away all the clouds that are hanging over the tops of the mountains.

> Don't ask what the world needs. Ask what makes
> you come alive, and go to it. Because what the world
> needs is people who have come alive.
>
> —Howard Thurman

It gives me an amazing feeling to stop during my day and be aware that I am connected to so many other people who are meditating and praying for peace.

When I stop and stay with this knowledge, I feel my breath becoming deeper and slower and filled with powerful energy. I can stay here as long as I choose and stop as often as I choose, bringing peace to more and more of my day.

> Today I am taking time to stop and feel
> my connection to all the people who are praying
> and meditating for world peace. This fills me with
> a deep sense of purpose and belonging and peace.

The fruit of silence is prayer.
The fruit of prayer is faith.
The fruit of faith is love.
The fruit of love is service.
The fruit of service is peace.
—Mother Teresa

Thee lift me and I'll lift thee and we'll ascend together.
—Quaker proverb

It is wonderful to know that wherever I am, the opportunity to make a difference is always there. Whether it is giving a smile to someone at the supermarket, praying for a sick friend, meditating for world peace, or making a donation to a local charity, I am always in a position to encourage peace.

By extending peace, I feel peace. By feeling peace, I extend peace. I can always make a difference in how I feel by breathing in peace. It feels so good to know that peace is as close as my next breath.

Today I am open to any opportunity
I have to pass peace on to others.

A life of reaction is a life of slavery,
intellectually and spiritually.

—Rita Mae Brown

If we are not willing to let go of the past, we react when something occurs that reminds us of the past and triggers old feelings. If we fear the future, we react when something occurs that triggers this fear. When we can learn to live in each moment, not filled with fears of the future or upsets and resentments from the past, we find peace.

By simply pausing before automatically responding, by slowing down and bringing our awareness to our breath, we can act in a way that is appropriate to what is actually going on in each moment. We can feel the presence of God and ask for guidance before making a hasty decision.

How freeing it is to pause before we respond to a memory or a fear. Only then are we free to act in each moment and make healthy, positive choices. In each moment we can act in ways that bring peace.

Today I am willing to slow down, to let go of everything that is keeping me from being fully present in each moment.

*Few find inner peace but this is not because they try
and fail, it is because they do not try.*
—Peace Pilgrim

Sometimes our activities can make us frantic. Without knowing it, we can let everyone and everything else run us. The phone rings and we run to answer it. Bills pile up and we're stressed with worry. A child needs this or that at the last minute. The school, library, doctor's appointment, work, church or synagogue, a neighbor, teacher, cousin, friend, mother, child, partner, or spouse—everyone's demands can become more important than our own inner needs.

Many a day is nonstop from morning to night, when we fall into bed completely exhausted. It is so important to take time to stop. Breathe. Slow down. Take a moment to relax. Be gentle with yourself.

The peace we have been looking for all along has always been in us; we just have to stop long enough to connect to it.

*Today I will examine all the demands and pressures I face,
taking time to see when I am putting unnecessary pressure
on myself. I am willing to let go of anything that really
isn't important and take some special time for me.*

Gratitude is our most direct line to God and the angels. The more we seek gratitude, the more reason the angels will give us for gratitude and joy to exist in our lives.
—Terry Lynn Taylor

I had been struggling with transferring all my files and programs onto a new computer and I was getting more and more frustrated as the days went by. It was an enormous job for me and it did not go smoothly. I was about to scream . . . again . . . when it hit me. What I was going through was so minute, so totally insignificant, compared to what other people are dealing with in the world. I felt small and ashamed.

I became overwhelmed with gratitude for all that I do have, realizing I have everything I need and so much more.

And I knew why I continue writing about peace. It is because I need to keep learning about it. I need to remind myself to live by what I know is true in my heart. I must keep practicing peace, one day at a time.

Even in times of great stress, I can accept what I am feeling without judgment, knowing God is with me and guiding me.

God is closest to those with broken hearts.
—*Jewish saying*

The pain that comes from the loss of someone or something we love can feel unbearable at times. We mourn when someone dear to us dies or when someone we love no longer loves us. We suffer if we lose a job that has had great meaning in our lives or if a dream that we have worked hard for falls apart. Our heart breaks when someone close to us comes down with a life-threatening disease or we find out we have one ourselves.

Just knowing there is a power greater than ourselves that we can turn to can bring us comfort and peace. Just as the sun is behind every cloud, whether or not we can see it, God is in our darkest nights, even when we forget. No matter what we are going through, this knowledge can soothe us, lighten our burden, ease our pain.

Whenever life is full of pain, I can still find peace with every breath I take, because I know God is with me.

The more anger towards the past you carry in your heart,
the less capable you are of loving in the present.
—Barbara De Angelis

Today, many of us have learned a great deal about what affects the way we feel. There are countless self-help books and magazine articles to guide us. Television has its share of gurus and experts who warn us to let go of our anger and resentments. Counselors, clergy, psychiatrists, social workers, psychologists, and Twelve-step Programs show us how.

Learning about it and doing something about it are two different things, however. We might think so-and-so doesn't deserve our forgiveness. "Look what he/she did to me! How can I possibly let go of my resentment after all I have been through?"

Buddhist teaching compares anger to a piece of burning coal: When you pick it up to throw it at someone else, you hurt your own hand most of all.

Anger blocks us from being in the present moment. It blocks us from feeling all the emotions of the present moment. It blocks us from love. It blocks us from peace.

Is it worth holding on to it?

Today I am willing to let go of any anger and resentment
that is keeping my heart closed to peace.

I am sending
peace
and
love
to
everyone
suffering
in the world
today.

> When you wonder what is coming, tell yourself the best
> is coming, the very best life and love have to offer,
> the best God and His universe have to send. Then open
> your hands to receive it. Claim it, and it is yours.
> —Melody Beattie

There might come a day when we just don't know what to do with ourselves. We might have days that we anticipate with dread. Perhaps we think there will be nothing to do and the day will be boring and dull. Maybe we anticipate trouble or misfortune.

On days when you are feeling this way, remember that we don't always have to have a plan for the day. Why not simply let the day take its course?

Have no expectations. Simply let it flow. Take each moment as it happens. Stay in the now.

Be mindful of every moment.

Experience each moment.

Feel alive with each moment. Expect the best from this day.

There is great freedom and peace when I choose to let God be
in charge of my day and expect the best. It feels so good to
know I have that choice.

Acceptance is the universal currency of real friendship.
It does not warp or shape or wrench a person to be
anything other than what they are.
—Joan Chittister

We begin by making friends with ourselves, accepting ourselves completely, with all our strengths and weaknesses. Then we can expand that acceptance to all those we love and then to all beings. Everyone. Everywhere. Regardless of race, color, sexual preference, nationality, or intelligence.

This is how we find peace in our hearts. This is our gift for ourselves. This is our gift to world peace.

God gives me all the willingness I need to let go of
my judgments. I can feel my heart filling with peace
and love as I practice acceptance.

To put the world in order, we must first put the nation in order; to put the nation in order, we must put the family in order; to put the family in order, we must cultivate our personal life; and to cultivate our personal life, we must first set our hearts right.
—Confucius

If we are holding on to anger, resentment, or fear, our hearts are blocked from feeling love and happiness. Often we are not even aware of what we are carrying within us; we just wonder why we don't feel more joyful. We go from day to day wondering if life will improve.

We may feel down and depressed or we may feel energized by our anger; either way, anger blocks our path to peace.

It's good to stop occasionally and take a personal inventory. Examine what it is that is keeping you from feeling at one with others, keeping you separated from God.

I am taking time today to ask God to remove anything that is blocking me from feeling peace in my heart. It feels so good to know that with God's help, I can be free.

How important is it?

I am rechecking my "to do" list today.

Is everything on it important?

Can I eliminate some things to make my day more peaceful?

Can I create an easier, softer day?

I am so grateful I can turn over my "to do" list to God and actually do only what God wants me to do today.

Whatever is going on
in my life today
can be
softened
when I make my choices
from
my
HEART.

A Sikh Prayer for Peace

God judges us according to our deeds, not the coat that we wear:
that Truth is above everything, but higher still is truthful living.
Know that we attain God when we love, and only *that* victory endures
in consequence of which no one is defeated.

The greatest challenge of the day is: how to bring about a revolution of the heart, a revolution which has to start with each one of us.
—Dorothy Day

So much of our praying focuses on the big picture of world peace. We pray for the safety of our soldiers. We pray for our politicians so that they may find peaceful means to end the problems of the world. We pray for things out there in the world to improve. Today, let's bring our awareness right here to ourselves and our own communities.

Just as we need to have peace within our own hearts before we can have peace in the world, we also need to have peace within our own communities before we can have peace in our country and before we can have peace in the world.

There is no way to exclude anyone if we truly want peace. Let's take some time today to focus first on what we can do to have peace within ourselves. Then let's take some time today to send peaceful messages to those in our own communities who don't live peacefully--even the child molesters and violent criminals. Let's not forget that peace will come one person at a time, one prayer at a time, one day at a time.

Today I am bringing my awareness to all the people in my community who harm others and keep us from being safe and at peace. I am sending prayers of loving kindness to them all.

The thing that is really hard, and really amazing, is giving up on being perfect and beginning to work on becoming yourself.
—Anna Quindlen

We often judge ourselves for not being perfect. Perhaps we've lost our temper or missed an appointment. Maybe we have forgotten a friend's birthday or have overeaten when we have committed to a diet. We can be angry at someone's anger or judge someone who is judgmental. Any one of these things, or the thousands of other things that can go wrong in a day, can lead us to beat ourselves up, call ourselves names, go into self-pity or even a depression.

We are simply imperfect human beings striving to be better. Our intention is what counts. Our intention is to improve, to be better, more loving, generous, and compassionate people. We are okay even when we overreact, make a mistake, or get angry. To find peace in our hearts, we must take a step back and treat ourselves with the same love and compassion we try to show others.

There is no room in our hearts for judgments!

Today I am going out of my way to accept that I am human.
I accept myself regardless of what I do, think, or say.
I accept myself completely and this brings me peace.

Relying on God has to begin all over again every day
as if nothing had yet been done.

—C. S. Lewis

I don't always wake up thinking of God, but when I do, it feels wonderful. No matter what kind of day I had the previous day, no matter what kind of sleep I had the night before, I still need positive, inspiring words to help connect me with God in the morning.

Meditation teacher Thich Nhat Hanh tells us that we have really arrived when we wake up knowing where we are in our breath cycle—on the in breath or the out breath. That is true awareness!

Breathing in is my connection to God.

Breathing out is my awareness to the universe and all the people in it.

Breathing in, I pray that I can feel this connection to God all day long.

Breathing out, I pray that I can feel this connection to all human beings all day long.

I am improving my conscious contact with God with prayer
and meditation. I know I am connected to God and all living
beings with every breath that I take.

Although the world is full of suffering,
it is full also of the overcoming of it.
—Helen Keller

There are times when it is difficult to get over a bad mood or get through a difficult time. Sadness lingers. Fear or self-pity keeps returning. We pray and meditate, talk to a spiritual advisor or sponsor, or do any one of a number of things that friends advise us to do and that have worked in the past. But there are times when it is difficult to feel peaceful, no matter what we do.

Maybe it's the fault of a full moon, or maybe someone looked at us the wrong way. Perhaps it's hormones, or our beloved pet has died. Perhaps we feel disconnected from our Higher Power or have had a disagreement with our best friend.

We may think that if we do "the right things" we'll feel good. This just isn't always true. Life has its ups and downs, storms and rainbows, floods and droughts, births and deaths. Even the most beautiful rose bushes lose their blossoms.

How, then, do we get through the down days, the dark times of our lives? By hanging in. By praying and meditating. By knowing that nothing is permanent and change is inevitable. By knowing that, we can handle anything for one moment, for one hour, for one day. By putting all our problems in God's hands.

By having faith that this, too, shall pass.

I know peace is on its way when
I turn my life over to the care of God.

44

I am still determined to be cheerful and happy, in whatever situation I may be; for I have learned from experience that the greater part of our happiness or misery depends upon our dispositions and not our circumstances.
                                        —Martha Washington

Somewhere deep inside of us there is a place that is quiet no matter what is going on. We can't always reach this place, but it is there. In painful times or fearful times it helps to know it is there and we can try to reach it.

Sitting quietly, being with our breath, we can stop the chattering of our mind and find this place, even if it is only for a moment.

It feels so good to know that God has given me an inner sanctuary where I can always go and find peace.

Today, as I remember
one thing
for which I am
grateful
I feel my
heart
SWELL
with
gratitude.

The game of life is the game of boomerangs. Our thoughts, deeds,
and words return to us sooner or later with astounding accuracy.
—Florence Scovel Shinn

I often walk in my neighborhood and there are many others who walk as well. It's a friendly community, and most people wave or say, "Nice day" or "Good morning" as they pass. Frequently I add a compliment, like "Nice outfit" or "Beautiful jacket" or "You look really good today!"

The person's face lights up and so does my heart!

We have the power to influence how another person feels, and that is a big responsibility! A thoughtless word or words said in anger can ruin a person's day. Giving vent to feelings of anger or resentment might help us feel better for the moment, but these feelings actually hurt us physically, emotionally, and spiritually. What we give to others we get back.

Notice how you feel when you give someone a compliment versus how you feel when you snap words that are hurtful. Then ask yourself how you would like to feel, and act accordingly.

Today I am looking for ways to make others smile
and this makes my own heart smile.

47

One day at a time.
    —*Twelve-step Program slogan*

Oh, how we ache for the world to be a better place! We feel pain in our hearts every time we pick up the newspaper or watch the evening news. Many of us cry when the sad faces of hungry, homeless children appear on the screen. We look, we listen, and we feel powerless to change the world.

But although we may feel powerless, we are not powerless. We can change part of the world . . . the part that begins in our hearts. We can change it with prayer and meditation. We can change it by smiling at a stranger, donating to an organization that supports peace, reading to the blind, becoming a mentor to a child, and in countless other ways that improve the quality of others' lives. One act of kindness each day makes a more peaceful world and a more peaceful us.

It feels so good to know that I am taking time today to do at least one thing to bring happiness to at least one other person.

I am strengthened
through the knowledge
that
God
is with me
and
I am with
God
wherever I go
today.

God sent each person into the world with a special message to deliver, a special song to sing, and a special act of love to bestow. No one else can speak my message or sing my song or offer my love . . . these are entrusted to me.
—Author unknown

Some of us sing our special song as soon as we are able to sing, while others struggle to find their song for many decades. The closer we come to knowing there is a power greater than ourselves who can guide us in our lives, the easier it is to sing.

We can connect with our song through prayer and meditation. Sometimes spending time in nature can help us open our hearts and discover what nurtures our souls. Sometimes a small voice inside whispers our next step. At other times, we hear a shout and we have no choice but to move forward.

Today I feel the joy of knowing that I have something special to do in this world and I trust I will know it when the time is right.

Your task is not to seek for love, but merely to seek and find all the barriers within yourself that you have built against it.
—Rumi

How do you find peace in your heart when you are angry? How do you find peace in your heart when you hold on to resentments?

You don't. No matter how often you meditate, take a walk, or take time to smell the flowers, an angry or resentful heart remains closed. Love and peace are locked out and only suffering remains.

So then the obvious question is, How can we let go of anger and resentment when we feel justified in being hurt or disappointed? How can we let go when all we want is revenge—when we want to hurt back?

It is not easy, but it is possible. We can pray for the willingness to let go. And if we aren't ready for this, we can pray for the willingness to be willing to let go. Just the slightest amount of willingness serves as a key to unlock a small door in our heart, and that opening will begin to stretch as our willingness grows.

And soon you will find the gift of peace in your heart, even when you're angry and resentful. It is God's precious gift to you in return for your willingness.

Today I will pray for the willingness to open my heart and let go of all the anger and resentments that have been keeping me stuck. Today I know that they only hurt me and keep me from feeling peaceful.

Joy is prayer—Joy is strength—Joy is love—
Joy is a net of love by which you can catch souls.
—*Mother Teresa*

What makes your heart swell?
What brings a lump to your throat?
What brings tears of happiness to your eyes?
What brings you joy?
Go out and find it today!

Today I am making a commitment to do at least one thing that
fills me with joy. Just thinking about it makes my heart smile!

The ability to simplify means to eliminate the unnecessary
so that the necessary may speak.
—Hans Hoffman

So many times we fill our lives with so much activity that there is no time left to just be. Busy from morning to night, rushing from here to there, we forget to stop, to breathe, and to connect with God. We forget to feed our souls. We forget what is really important in our lives.

Perhaps you are a people pleaser and can't say no. Perhaps you are afraid to be quiet for fear of what might be there in the silence. Perhaps you think everything depends on you and you rush to fix this and fix that, do this and do that, so that everything will be fine and everyone will be happy.

Find some time today to stop. Turn off all phones and TVs and radios and music players. Stop and just be. Breathe. Be still.

Take inventory of all you do in your life. Look at everything and examine whether it is really important. What isn't being accomplished that is important? What are you doing to please others that takes up too much of your time? What can you let go? What is really important?

You'll be amazed to discover how much peace will be in your life when you are willing to simplify.

Today I am finding some time to stop and take inventory of what is really important in my life. I am willing to begin to simplify.

They say the chains of habit are too light to be felt until they are too heavy to be broken. The chains you put around yourself now have enormous consequences as you go through life.
—Warren Buffett

This might be a good day to look at the habits that fill your time and thoughts, drain your energy, and keep you stuck. What do you think you can't live without? Coffee? Alcohol? Drugs? Gambling? Shopping? TV? E-mail? Sex? Or the less obvious habits such as the need for excitement, drama, being right, new clothes, computer games?

Many times we don't realize that we are hooked on something we like. We think we can give it up any time.

Why not try it today? Give up something you enjoy for a week or two. See how you feel. See how often you think about this during the day. Notice how often your mind goes to it. Notice how much space it takes up in your attention. How much energy it drains from your life.

Before long, the perceived need for your habit will dissipate. Once it does, you will notice the extra time you have in your days and in your thoughts. Notice the peace you have when your energy isn't spent on your habit.

Today I am examining any habit I have that takes up time and space and energy. I am willing to let go of this habit so I can be free and feel the peace of each moment.

Life is what is happening when you're busy making other plans.
—John Lennon

I used to wake up in the morning and, before even getting out of bed, think about all the things I had to do that day. I was already tired without even moving my body. Before I learned a better way, I would go over and over my "to do" list, and then I would work on my budgets. First I would think over the personal budget and all the bills that had to be paid, trying to figure out where the money would come from. Then the mental work for my company budget would begin. In no time, I would become filled with hopelessness because my "to do" list had grown even more overwhelming.

Thank goodness for prayer and meditation! For many years they have replaced those first morning thoughts. I no longer dread beginning my day.

*Today I am willing to let go of my "to do" list
and begin my days connecting with God. I begin each
day with thoughts of peace and love.*

And yet not choice but habit rules the unreflecting herd.
—William Wordsworth

There is a story about a woman who always cut the ends off each roast before placing it in a pan. One day her daughter asked why she did so, and she responded that she didn't really know; it was something her mother had always done. She asked her own mother why she had always cut the ends off a roast prior to placing it in the pan. Her mother answered it was something she'd always watched her mother do. Finally, the woman asked her grandmother. "Oh, that," replied the elderly woman. "My roast pan was small. I always had to cut the ends off to make it fit!"

When you think about the things you do over and over again, you may want to reconsider why you do them. Perhaps you saw it done that way in your family. Perhaps it's just a habit. Perhaps it's time to change!

Today I am taking a fresh look at everything
I do on autopilot. I am opening myself to the freedom
of finding new ways to live my life.

Every memorable act in the history of the world is a triumph of enthusiasm. Nothing great was ever achieved without it because it gives any challenge or any occupation, no mater how frightening or difficult, a new meaning . . . with it you can accomplish miracles.
—Og Mandino

Let's make this a very special day for world peace.

Imagine the world as a very safe place where people can be free to be who they are. Let this enthusiasm pour through you so you can really feel it through your entire body. Now carry these feelings into your goal of world peace. Feel the excitement, the possibilities, the wonder of what this would mean. The end of suffering. The end of wars. Just thinking about this is spreading powerful, peaceful, exciting energy out into the world!

Today I am filled with enthusiasm and excitement as I spread the energy of peace out into the world!

And Jabez called on the Lord of Israel saying,
"Oh that You would bless me indeed,
and enlarge my territory,
that Your hand would be with me,
and that You would keep me from evil,
that I may not cause pain!"
So God granted him what he requested.
—1 Chronicles 4:10

All the energies
of the
Universe
are with me
as I
move
through
this
day.
This fills me
with
great
peace.

When I despair, I remember that all through history the way of truth and love has always won. There have been tyrants and murderers and for a time they seem invincible but in the end, they always fall—think of it, always.
—Mahatma Gandhi

These wise words can help us through earthquakes and hurricanes, sickness and pain, suicide bombings and wars. Whenever we are feeling defeated and ready to give up, let's remember them.

When it looks as if we are at the end of our rope, when all hope seems lost, let us remember that truth and love always win.

No matter what is going on in my life today, I can choose to feel the strength of the knowledge that truth and love will always prevail.

The path that does not run away but embraces our
suffering is the path that will lead us to liberation.
—The Buddha

It is normal not to want to face feelings of pain and despair. It is normal to want to push away feelings of disappointment and failure. It is normal to want to change unpleasant feelings to pleasant ones. The problem is that when we don't face and experience our feelings, they stay buried within us and keep us stuck. They block our ability to feel love and compassion towards ourselves and others.

We might hide from our unwanted feelings in ways that are obvious, such as drinking or taking drugs. But there are many ways we hide without even being aware that this is what we are doing. Perhaps we work too much or stay very busy in other ways. Perhaps we spend hours in front of the television. One woman told me she had become aware that all her reading was an escape from emotions she didn't want to feel.

As difficult as it might seem, feeling our feelings is the only way we can move beyond them and grow. Allowing ourselves to feel our suffering and giving ourselves love and support and compassion can soften our hearts and diminish our fears. Being gentle with ourselves lessens the strain of difficult times and keeps us from being stuck in our suffering.

It feels so empowering to know that I can get through
anything that comes my way with the help of my Higher
Power. As long as I don't run away from my feelings,
I can experience peace in the middle of adversity.

When you blame others, you give up your power to change.
—Dr. Robert Anthony

Maybe the dog really did eat your homework! Maybe you really did run out of gas. Maybe he really was rude to you and she really did come in first because she cheated. Maybe you didn't have loving parents. Maybe you couldn't afford to go to college. All these and many more excuses might be perfectly true. But if you focus on the excuses—if you insist on blaming people and circumstances for your unhappiness—you stay stuck in a field of weeds. You may never see the flowers.

If you are ever to feel the peace that lies under all your resentments, you must let go of the weeds, one by one. You can pray for willingness to let go and to forgive. And if you're not ready to take that step, you can pray to be willing to be willing.

Once you experience the freedom that results from letting go of anger and resentments, you will never want to hold on to them again!

How much do you really want peace?

I pray for the willingness today to let go of anything that is holding me back from feeling peace in my heart.

FEAR = *False Evidence Appearing Real*
—*Author unknown*

Fear is natural and healthy. Fear can save our lives. When a car drifts unexpectedly into our lane, we swerve quickly to avoid an accident. When something threatens us, fear shouts at us to take self-protective action.

But so many of our fears are born in our thoughts and not in reality. We project our fears into a future that does not exist. We imagine scenes where the worst happens. We make ourselves physically ill by stressing our bodies with scenarios that exist only in our own minds.

How much gentler to ourselves can we be when we learn to say no to our projected thoughts, to stay in the present moment where we can shine a light upon reality. That way our fears have no place to go. Then each moment can become a moment of peace rather than a moment of stress.

I am so grateful to know that I can live in the reality of each moment, knowing God is with me and guiding me.

The more I work with people and the more I go through life, the more I realize that people just want to be happy. If I take five minutes out of each day to remember to treat people the same way I want to be treated, we can accomplish wonderful things together.
—Bob Fishel

It is often little things that make us happy and bring happiness to others. A warm greeting or compliment can bring a smile to someone's face and, in turn, put a smile on our own. A question about a loved one or a show of interest in someone's pet project lets that person know we care.

Our goal is to treat everyone with respect. Sympathizing with someone's difficulties or encouraging someone's success does wonders for everyone involved. We all benefit when we treat others the way we want to be treated, and our world becomes a more peaceful place.

Today I find peace and happiness as I remember to treat others the way I want to be treated.

Take a moment right now to stop and breathe.
Notice what you are feeling.
Bring your awareness to
this
very
moment.
Are you rushing to read this, just to get through it
and move on to the next thing on your
"to do" list?
Are you thinking of all you have
to do today?
Or
are
you
slowing
down

taking time

feeling peaceful?
The choice is yours.

In our daily lives, we must see that it is not happiness that makes us grateful, but the gratefulness that makes us happy.
—Albert Clarke

Often we think we will be happy when we get this or that: the new job, the new home, the special someone. And we are . . . for a while. But then we are ready for something else, and something else and something else.

There have been times when I have felt hopeless and depressed and deprived. However, when I have had the ability, the vision, and the willingness to focus on something I *do* have and for which I feel gratitude, my energy-draining emotions melt and I feel joy in my heart. My spirit lifts and the feelings of hopelessness, depression, or deprivation melt away.

Today I am focusing on at least one thing for which I am grateful. It is amazing how much peace this brings me!

*Watch your manner of speech if you wish
to develop a peaceful state of mind. Start each day
by affirming peaceful, contented, and happy attitudes,
and your days will tend to be pleasant and successful.*
—Norman Vincent Peale

We can feel ourselves soften when we move our attention from self-defeating thoughts to our hearts, where love lives. Our minds empty and rest in these moments, and we find peace.

Practicing this on a regular basis makes it easier to find peace when stress and conflict creep into our minds and into our lives. The more often we practice, the easier it becomes. Eventually it becomes automatic. When stress arrives, we become aware of our self-talk and we move our focus to our hearts instead.

Staying in our negative thoughts creates unpleasant emotions. Moving into our hearts creates peace. And we deserve to feel peaceful!

*Today I am bringing my conscious awareness into a place
where I can find love and peace. Today I turn to my heart.*

Gratitude opens our minds and hearts. It instantly connects us to the present moment. Plus, it feels absolutely wonderful. The fact that gratitude is so easy to come by gives us one more reason to be grateful.

—Raphael Cushnir

I am taking some time
NOW
to think of one person who has made a
positive difference in my life.
I am taking time . . .
NOW
to let my heart fill with gratitude
for this person.
I am taking time . . .
NOW
to feel
FULL
of gratitude.

It is wonderful to know that I can stop at any time and find joy in my heart when I think of someone for whom I am grateful.

The miracle comes quietly into the mind
that stops an instant and is still.
—A Course in Miracles

There was a time when I thought I was the only one in the world with thoughts that went on and on. It was not until I learned to quiet my mind with meditation that I discovered it was normal for human beings to have racing minds. This racing mind has been called a "monkey mind" in which our thoughts are like monkeys endlessly jumping from branch to branch.

However, we can train our thoughts and tame our monkey minds. We begin simply by sitting quietly, becoming aware of our breath as it goes in and goes out. Watching our thoughts as they come in and go out and then returning to our breathing, we will be amazed at how quickly we will begin to feel peaceful and how quickly our world will change for the better.

Today I feel the miracle of peace as I take time to sit quietly
and meditate. It feels so good to be in this stillness.

A Native African Prayer for Peace

Almighty God, the Great Thumb we cannot evade to tie any knot; the Roaring Thunder that splits mighty trees: the all-seeing Lord up on high who sees even the footprints of an antelope on a rock mass here on Earth. You are the one who does not hesitate to respond to our call. You are the cornerstone of peace.

> God grant me the serenity
> To accept the things I cannot change;
> The courage to change the things I can;
> And the wisdom to know the difference.
> —Reinhold Niebuhr

How can we keep the bad moods of other people from affecting us? How can we keep our own serenity when there is chaos and stress all around us?

One way is to keep this serenity prayer close by, to know that we cannot change other persons, places, or things, and to understand and accept that we can change only ourselves.

And we can pray for the wisdom to really know this in all situations.

> Today I trust that when I ask, God gives me the wisdom
> to know that I am responsible for my own feelings,
> guiding me to know that I can change only myself.

Every sixty seconds you spend angry, upset, or mad is a full minute of happiness you'll never get back.
—Author unknown

We claim we want to feel peaceful but we often hold on to our anger.

We pray to have peace in our hearts but our resentments can keep us up at night.

We struggle for balance and happiness and yet so many times we don't accept life on life's terms.

Why not try a happiness-and-peace experiment today? Have a piece of paper and pencil with you. Stop and notice when you get upset. Jot down the source. Be mindful of any time you get angry. Jot down the source. Notice whether the feeling of anger or upset came from a thought that triggered a memory that then triggered the feeling, or whether an actual event triggered the feeling. Just notice it and jot it down. No judgments! You're on a learning mission today.

If you have time when these situations occur, examine each one as it occurs and decide whether or not you want to hold on to these feelings. If you are busy, look at your paper at the end of the day. Many times we hold on to negative or unpleasant feelings just because that's what we've always done. Now you can change. Try letting go more quickly by talking about your feelings, writing about them, or asking yourself how important they really are. Then, as your willingness increases, you'll be amazed to find your peace and happiness increase in direct proportion.

Today I am taking an honest look at how long I hold on to my upsets. I pray for the willingness to let go more quickly so I can have more peace and happiness in my life.

STOP

BREATHE

SMILE

SIGH

Put your appreciation into action by taking time to show your appreciation. Tell one or more people something you appreciate about them. Remember, what you put out comes back.
—Doc Childre and Sara Paddison

We all want to be valued and appreciated. Knowing how good we feel when someone appreciates us, we can feel that way again when we give someone else the same gift.

It is so easy to change a bad mood to a good mood just by showing how much we appreciate someone. Showing our appreciation can also mend a relationship with someone with whom we are having difficulty. Or it can open the door to a deeper connection with someone in the future.

Each person we touch with our appreciation will be in a better mood too, at least for that moment. This better mood is usually contagious, so others receive the benefit of it in a chain of interconnectedness.

Today I will show my appreciation to at least one other person, enjoying the knowledge that as I do this, positive energy is flowing out into the world and back to me.

> There are two ways
> of spreading light:
> to be the candle
> or the mirror that reflects it.
> —Edith Wharton

I absolutely do make a difference in this world.
Every thought, feeling, and action makes a difference.
I know I can change one negative thought, feeling, or action
to a positive one today and make a positive
difference in this world!

> Today I am sending powerful, peaceful energy
> out into the universe. It feels so good knowing
> that I DO make a positive difference!

If there is light in the soul,
there will be beauty in the person.
If there is beauty in the person,
there will be harmony in the house.
If there is harmony in the house,
there will be order in the nation.
If there is order in the nation,
there will be peace in the world.
—Chinese proverb

Peace of mind is that mental condition
in which you have accepted the worst.
—Lin Yü-t'ang

"Accepting the worst" might be the last advice you'd be willing to heed, but it holds the key to maintaining a peaceful presence in the face of life's greatest challenges. Really, what is "the worst?" Our ego needs the world to show up in a certain way to feel safe and in control. But life's most difficult events—sickness, death, and so on—are often beyond our control. We may have played a part in their creation, but when they arise all we can do is see that God is present and allow our souls to grow from the lessons they hold.

To understand there is only One Presence in the universe is to see God in all creation, even the things that we don't understand or that frighten us. To understand that we are a part of that Presence is to recognize that, regardless of what happens in the physical world, our spiritual essence is untouchable. Only when we cease struggling and accept what is, can we access the latent spiritual power within and begin to see the blessings that hide within life's challenges. Then, even in the "worst," we can transform everything into an opportunity for our souls to grow, and we can say with surety, "All things contribute to the calm peace of my soul."

Submitted by Rev. Steve Carty Cordry, Unity minister

All things contribute to the calm peace of my soul.

So watch the thought and its ways with care, and let it
spring from love, born out of concern for all beings.
—The Buddha

Whatever it is that I feel in my heart I pass on to others, knowingly or unknowingly. As I grow in my awareness of what is going on in my mind, I can direct my thoughts. This is so powerful! I can choose to feel peaceful and create an atmosphere of peace for myself and those around me. I can then send that feeling out into the universe, making a difference in the world.

Today I am taking time to fill my heart with joy
and love and compassion, sending them out to everyone
in the world with a prayer for peace.

Lord, make me a blessing to someone today.
—Jan Karon

I smiled when I read this quote, and a lump rose in my throat. What a beautiful thought! Just to go through the day mindful that there is someone I might meet whom I can help is a magnificent goal!

I felt warm and secure in the fact that this is purpose enough. To be present. To be willing to be there for someone else. To pass on a message of hope or peace or healing. Perhaps simply to give my full attention to something that someone is saying.

I am confident that I will know what to do when the situation presents itself as long as I stay open to the knowledge that I am being guided.

Today I am ready and eager to be a blessing for someone and I feel blessed with this knowledge.

The sun doesn't stop shining because some people are blind.
—*Mark Nepo*

Just because some people can't see the path to peace does not mean it is not there. Just because some people don't realize that killing does not create peace does not mean it is not true.

Those of us who know in our hearts that love, forgiveness, and compassion are the stepping-stones to peace are so blessed! We can choose to feel love instead of hate and peace instead of anger.

Today I choose to practice love, forgiveness,
and compassion every chance I get. I am so grateful
that my heart is full of peace and love.

Peace is inevitable to those who offer peace.
—A Course in Miracles

To have the goal of world peace is so extraordinary that many people might think it is too huge to even consider. The thought is so enormous it can be overwhelming; the goal is so enormous it may seem impossible, something that could never happen in our lifetime.

But how do we know that praying and meditating for peace won't work if we don't try it? How do we know that one more prayer, my prayer or your prayer, could not shift the energy of the universe to create the critical mass needed for world peace? What if it were up to me or you and we chose not to get involved?

---

*Today, no matter what my mind tells me,
I am meditating for world peace.*

Life lived for tomorrow will always be just a day away.
—Leo Buscaglia

It is common for young children on a long trip to ask repeatedly, "Are we there yet?" impatiently waiting for the promised destination. They are often oblivious to all the sights they are passing along the way. When we do the same thing as adults, focusing on the future, anxiously waiting to be in our new home, job, or relationship, we too miss out on the life that is happening along the way. We fail to discover the peace that is found when we live in each moment, in each breath.

We are alive in this moment now. Don't wait for some future event, thinking that it will make you happy. Stop and experience your life now.

*Today I am fully experiencing the peace
in each moment as I breathe in and out, bringing
my awareness to the miracle of being alive.*

What we create within is mirrored outside us.
This is the law of the universe.
—Shakti Gawain

We could be in a meadow filled with glorious wildflowers, or watching a magnificent sunset, but if our hearts are filled with anger or resentment, we will not feel peace. On the other hand, we could be in the midst of a hurricane and feel peace, if we have peace in our hearts.

While what is going on outside of us can certainly cause fear and confusion, we can transform those emotions to peace through prayer and meditation. The closer we are to God, the more quickly our negative and destructive emotions leave us and we feel peace.

Today I am opening my heart and inviting God
into my life. Then, no matter what transpires,
I can go into my heart and find peace.

Between stimulus and response there is a space.
In that space lies our freedom and power to choose our response.
In those choices lie our growth and happiness.
—Viktor Frankl

One way we can find inner peace is by becoming mindful of how we respond to persons, places, and things. If we allow ourselves to respond automatically, as we have always done before, we can be filled with anger, fear, jealousy, and all the negative emotions that have pulled us down in the past. Instead, when a new situation occurs that pushes our buttons, we can stop, be mindful of how we are feeling, and choose to feel peace.

For example, if someone demeans or insults us, we can hear the words but choose not to take them in where they can hurt us. The words are merely someone else's opinion, and that does not mean they are true. We can choose, instead, to take a conscious breath, which creates a new space and gives us time to slow down our reactions. In that space we can make a conscious choice as to how we want to respond.

Today I am mindful of whatever triggers my emotions,
and I choose peaceful reactions whenever possible.

*We look forward to the time when the power of Love
will replace the love of Power. Then will the world
know the blessings of Peace.*
—William Ewart Gladstone

I have great power today . . . the power of my mind! I can sit and think about this power and guide it to thoughts of peace. I can feel this peace in my heart. I can think about peace for all the people in the world and send peace from my heart out to everyone. I can encourage someone else to think about peace for all the people in the world today, and together we can make that happen!

*It is such a powerful feeling knowing that I am connected
with so many other people who are bringing peace into their
own hearts and then sending peace out into the world.*

*Because thoughts come from the inside, not the outside,
what we think determines what we see.*

—Jane Nelson

Changing thoughts from "What is wrong with me?" to "What is right with me?" can make all the difference in the world in how we feel. Finding just one good thing about ourselves releases tension held by negative thoughts and can even make us smile. Our whole attitude changes. We become open, relaxed, and peaceful. We can even feel joy.

By learning the difference between what is real and what is imagined, we can discover that just because we think something, that does not necessarily make it true.

Today I am stopping whenever I think of myself in a negative way and I am focusing on one good quality. I find peace and serenity knowing that my negative thoughts are merely words, blocking me from the peace and love that I was born to feel.

I will have peace if I treat others peacefully.
—*Karen Casey*

Have you ever really stopped and examined your feelings when a driver cuts in front of you and then drives slower than the speed limit? Or when the person in front of you has thirty items in a twelve-item checkout line in the supermarket? Notice your feelings the next time someone does something that is frustrating. Don't think of the other person. Think of yourself and bring your awareness to how you are feeling. Your breath might be shallow. Your fist or your jaw might be clenched.

This is a perfect time to practice mindfulness. Observe all that is going on for you without any judgments. Completely accept what you are feeling. Be aware of your reactions. As you do this, you will notice a shift in your feelings. The anger and frustration will leave and you will feel your body relax. You will feel peaceful and be less tempted to treat the other person with anger.

I am practicing the art of mindfulness as I go through my day today. I am the observer, not the judge, as I bring peace to myself and others.

The degree of harmony that comes into your experience is proportional to the degree of your spiritual development.
—Joel Goldsmith

Each time we take another step toward living by spiritual principles, we experience more and more harmony in our lives. The joy and the peace we feel when we practice forgiveness, compassion, and generosity teach us that this is the way we want to live our lives. Why would anyone choose to live with the tension of anger, resentment, and judgments if he or she could feel peace instead?

The gifts of harmony and peace are a direct result of our spiritual thoughts and actions.

Today God is guiding me to be willing to make spiritual choices in my life. Today I am experiencing peace.

How can we find peace?
The answer is written within the word

PEACE:

Practice
Empathy
And
Compassion
Everywhere

Submitted by Steffi L. Shapiro, holistic psychotherapist and yoga teacher

---

Each day I take time to find the peace that is within me and then take time to share it with others.

God is here, now, awaiting our request for help. Asking will result in a wave of peacefulness followed by a sense of well-being that will not leave us as long as we keep our hearts open to God.
—Karen Casey

Days do not always go the way we would like them to go. Jobs are lost. Earthquakes and hurricanes hit. Relationships break up. We fall ill. People dear to us die.

Even in times of deep despair, when we remember that there is a power greater than ourselves guiding us and carrying us, we can rest in the comfort and peace of that knowledge. We can get through these times knowing that there is a higher purpose, even though it may not be revealed for some time.

No matter what is going on in my life today,
I can keep my heart open, knowing that God is with me.
I can find peace in prayer.

Namaste

I honor the place in you
in which the entire universe dwells.
I honor the place in you which is of
love, of truth, of light, of peace.
When you are in that place in you,
and I am in that place in me,
we are one.

I am taking time
right now to

STOP

BREATHE

feel my breath
flow into my heart
and
feel
the
peace.

Nothing weighs on us so heavily as a secret.
—Jean de La Fontaine

Imagine everyone reading this book telling the truth about something he has been keeping to himself. Imagine everyone revealing a secret she has buried, perhaps from shame, guilt, or even loyalty. Now imagine the relief everyone feels as this powerful force that has been blocked is released to flow out into the universe.

Secrets are heavy burdens that pull us down, stealing our energy, blocking our love, limiting our relationship with God. We may feel angry, depressed, tired, numb, or afraid when we hide our secrets.

Is there something you are hiding? Take a risk! Reveal a secret to a trusted friend, spiritual advisor, mentor, or sponsor today. You will feel such freedom and peace. You are worth it!

*Today God gives me all the courage I need to share something
I have been hiding. Peace is my reward. I am worth it!*

I will take at least a few minutes . . .
NOW
to find at least one thing that I have for which
to be thankful.
At least five minutes . . .
NOW
to let my heart fill.
At least five minutes . . .
NOW
to feel FULL.

It is wonderful
to know that
I
can
replace
any negative emotion
with joy
and
peace
by simply
shifting my thoughts
to something
for which I
am
grateful.

Thoughts become things . . . choose the good ones!
—*Mike Dooley*

Peaceful thoughts take practice. We won't just wake up one day and find that all thoughts of fear, anger, resentment, anxiety, and the like have left us. The truth is, most of us will never be completely free of negative and destructive thoughts, but we can have them less and less often. When we become aware of a thought that isn't peaceful, we can choose to notice it, gently accept that we have such a thought, and then say STOP! We can bring our awareness to our hearts, where we feel love, and think of something peaceful, or we can turn our awareness to the God of our understanding.

In time, this new way of reacting will feel more natural and become a habit. In time it may become automatic. The rewards of feeling peaceful and knowing that peaceful energy is flowing out into the universe are beyond all imagination.

I am watching my thoughts today, careful not to hang on to anything that is blocking my heart from peace.

*How can you follow the course of
your life if you do not let it flow?*

—Lao-tzu

Most of us are unaware of the blocks we carry that keep us from feeling our true purpose. Messages from the past, such as "You'll never amount to anything," "You'd better marry rich so your husband can take care of you," or "There's nothing you can do about it. It's all predetermined" are buried so deep, we often can't see their effect on us.

As we become willing to look deeply, with the intention to live fully and to allow our soul's purpose to unfold, jolts of awareness will come to us. To live fully, we must be willing to let go of all the negative, self-defeating messages of the past and create our own loving messages for each moment.

*With God's help I am replacing all my negative thoughts
with self-affirming messages of peace and love. It feels so
good to know that I can love and respect myself today!*

Anger will never disappear so long as thoughts of resentment are cherished in the mind. Anger will disappear just as soon as thoughts of resentment are forgotten.
—The Buddha

It's obvious that we can't feel peaceful when we are angry. It's also obvious that we will stay angry when we hold on to thoughts of resentment. If this is so obvious, why do we do it? For so many reasons!

One reason is that we want to be right. Another is that we want be acknowledged for our pain or the injustices we have suffered. Perhaps it simply feels good to have the energy of anger. Perhaps, unconsciously, we hold on in order to have someone to blame for our inadequacies or our failures, not realizing that we are keeping ourselves in the victim role by holding on.

The time to let go of our resentment is now. Only then can we find the peace we so deeply seek.

I am so grateful that God is giving me the willingness to let go of all my resentments so I can feel peace.

A Jewish Prayer for Peace

Come, let us go up to the mountain of the Lord, that we may walk the paths of the Most High. And we shall beat our swords into ploughshares, and our spears into pruning hooks. Nation shall not lift up sword against nation, neither shall they learn war any more. And none shall be afraid, for the mouth of the Lord of Hosts has spoken.

With understanding you will become compassionate,
and that will change everything.
—Thich Nhat Hanh

The more I begin to understand myself, the more compassion I have for myself. The more I understand myself, the more I am able to understand others. Human beings all share the same basic need for food, safety, shelter, and community. We all want to be loved and to be treated with respect.

When I think in these terms about someone I might have considered my enemy, my fear or anger softens and compassion creeps into my heart.

Today I am letting God open my heart so that I can find
willingness to see my enemy with the eyes of compassion.
This is the only way I can find peace.

A donkey with a load of holy books is still a donkey.
—Sufi saying

We can read about peace.

We can write about peace.

We can talk about peace.

But until we take the steps to develop inner peace, we will not be peaceful. Our intention and our willingness are only the beginning of a journey towards inner peace. The next step is a commitment, followed by daily practice.

How committed are you?

Nothing stands in my way of my
daily practice for inner peace today.

No matter how well we have prepared,
the moment belongs to God.

—Sheldon Kopp

There is only so much I can control. I can give this day everything I have. I can give my utmost attention and commitment to at least five minutes today spent meditating for peace in the world. I can carry this thought, this feeling, with me and express it in all my actions to the best of my ability for the rest of the day.

I can feel the great power of the thought that I am joining with so many others with the same intention.

Today I will do my very best to bring peace to my life and to the lives around me and then to accept the outcome.

It feels so good to know that my best is good enough!
I am doing the best I can and God is in charge of the results.

If we learn to open our hearts, anyone, including the
people who drive us crazy, can be our teacher.
—Pema Chödrön

What can we possibly learn from the driver who cuts us off or the rude person behind the counter or the friend who forgets our birthday? So much! What we learn is not about them but about ourselves. When we take a close look at how we respond to these people, we can discover our character defects, our habits, our automatic responses that block us from feeling peace.

Does it do us any good to get angry at the driver who is now creeping along at twenty miles an hour in front of us?

We might see the rude person behind the counter for only five minutes in our entire life. Is it worth carrying our upset with us for the rest of the day?

So our birthday isn't the most important thing on our friend's mind and she forgot to send us a card. Is this worth resenting our friend and feeling disturbed when we see her?

How important are most things that cause us pain and suffering? If we decide to change our automatic reactions, we can replace them with the question, "What can I learn about me from this person or this situation?"

Why not use today as a practice day to grow spiritually? Be mindful of how you feel and what you think, whom you judge and what upsets you. Open your heart to everyone you meet. Stop, breathe, and feel the peace.

I am becoming more peaceful as I learn and accept that it is
I, not others, who create my suffering. I am opening my
heart to everyone I meet today.

If enough of us do our little bit, after all, then added together
we do make a difference. The whole is the sum of its parts.
—Terry Tillman

As I stop today, in this time that I have committed to world peace, I can discover at least one thing that will change my life and thus affect the lives of those around me.

It does not have to be big or great. One thing to make my life more peaceful. Just one thing. One small thing. I do make a difference!

Today I know that any action I take that comes from peace
and love has a ripple effect on the entire world!

Words are very powerful.
Words have the POWER to MOVE us
from a place very deep within us.
Words have the POWER to SHIFT us
from old beliefs to new ones.
Words have the POWER to INSPIRE us
to take action steps that make a difference.
Words have the POWER to SHAKE US UP
and help us change!
Words have the POWER to TOUCH our hearts
and bring us peace.

Through community, through those who hold the energy that keeps us awake, we can tune in and ask God for guidance. No individual knows everything, but God does. Spiritual community reminds us that we are connected.

—Mary Manin Morrissey

Imagine countless numbers of people with goals of deepening their inner peace. Imagine countless numbers of people committed to sending this peaceful energy out into the world. We are joined together in our hearts, in our intentions, and in our commitments.

All of us reading this page today are truly a community.

It is so heartwarming to know that I am not alone, that I am joined with so many other people who are as committed as I am to personal peace and world peace.

Meditation is a form of acknowledging your connection with the spirit of universal love, and it allows a sense of peace and love to flood your being. The tranquility that follows stays with you, reducing stress and promoting a state of awareness throughout the day.

—Ruth Ross

As we let ourselves relax and let stress leave our bodies, we open up to more and more tranquility and peace. The more we open and let go of our stress, the more room we make to be filled with peace and love, and we carry that with us throughout our day.

I stop today and take the time to be still and be in touch with my Higher Power. I feel myself filling with love and peace as I relax and let go of the stress in my day, and I pass this peace on to others.

*The key to a passionate life is to trust
and follow the energy within us.*
—Shakti Gawain

As we begin to slow down, to take this time each day, we begin to quiet our minds. In this process we discover the very traits that have blocked our energy. We come face-to-face with our fears, our resistance, and our denial. And as we accept what we see, without judgment but with gratitude, we can actually feel new energies being released. Trust this new energy. It is part of a bigger picture, a higher level of spirituality. It will bring change on a grander scale to a world that so badly needs it.

Today I am willing to let go of all the negative patterns that block me from my truth. And as I let go, I trust and follow a powerful new energy that is guiding me and all the world's people to a higher purpose!

A Navajo Indian Prayer for Peace

Before me peace,

Behind me peace,

Under me peace,

Over me peace,

All around me peace.

Today's Peaceful Exercise

Today I am bringing my full awareness to a daily routine.

I am being mindful of every aspect of washing the dishes.

I am aware of the touch of the water and how it feels when the basin is filled with suds.

I am aware of the smell of the soap and how it feels when I wash a dish.

I am aware of the sound of the water as it pours from the faucet.

I am aware of the sight of the water and the soap.

If thoughts take me away from my awareness, I simply notice them and return my attention to my routine.

This quiets my mind and gives me great peace.

I am carrying this peace with me for the rest of the day.

Thou shalt not be a victim.
Thou shalt not be a perpetrator.
Above all, thou shalt not be a bystander.
—Yehuda Bauer

Today we know that we have choices.

We can take a stand.

We can say YES!

We can say NO!

We can stop and wait for inner guidance.

We can take whatever steps are necessary

for inner peace.

We can make a difference!

We do make a difference!

I am so grateful that God is guiding me to make positive, loving, and peaceful decisions today, not only for me but for the people around me.

The longest journey is the journey inward,
for he who has chosen his destiny has started upon
his quest for the source of his being.
—Dag Hammarsjköld

We have often looked to other people, places, and things for answers.

We thought others could free the world of wars, pain, pollution, starvation, disease, homelessness, and ignorance.

It is time to begin to trust that small voice within, coming from the person we really are. It is time to look within and begin to uncover all that has been blocking us from our truth, from our strength, from our wisdom, from our Higher Power. It is time to discover our own power and participate in the healing of our world!

I am beginning to feel my own personal power today!

When we discover the still, quiet place that lies within each of us, we can see it as a base to untangle ourselves from the doubt, indecision, ill health, guilt, and other forms of old programming that result in confused and defused actions.
—Hallie Iglehart

As you dare to see that you have been ruled by old programming, know that new truths and positive, healthy thoughts are replacing the negative ones! Know that you are in the process of moving forward, and in that process you are helping others in this universe to move forward.

Miracles begin to happen when we sit still and begin to look within. Let those miracles be there for you today!

I am clearing out old confusion and doubt so that I can see the miracles today and participate in the recovery of the universe.

In troubled times it is hard to feel peaceful.
In difficult times it is hard to feel peaceful.
I can take time to allow myself to be with thoughts
of peace no matter what I am going through today.
I can take time and fill myself with peaceful energy
no matter what else I am feeling today.

When you have learned how to decide with God, all decisions become as easy and as right as breathing. There is no effort and you will be led as gently as if you were being carried down a quiet path in summer.

—*A Course in Miracles*

Peace comes when I let God guide my life.
Peace comes when I know I am not in charge.
Peace comes when I pray for direction
  and I follow what I know to be true.
Peace comes and I pass it on.

Today I am doing my very best to bring peace to my life and to the lives around me by trusting God's guidance.

I am taking time today to find
at least one thing that I have for which to
be thankful.
Time today . . . to let my heart fill.
Time today . . . to feel
FULL
of
peace.

> Nobody could make a greater mistake than he who did
> nothing because he could only do a little.
> —Edmund Burke

We hear and see so much sadness and pain in the news that eventually we can become desensitized to it. Two hundred killed by the Taliban. Two thousand killed in an earthquake. A father kills his children. A son kills his father. Six million Jews. . . . Hundreds of thousands of people in Darfur. . . . We can easily become immune to the next disaster. Or we can feel powerless because the situation seems too huge for us to do anything about.

However, we can make a difference. We do make a difference. Just look back at history. Sweatshops no longer exist in many countries. Women now vote in most countries. Changes have taken place in the world because of the vision and determination of people who would not let injustices continue. They could not be peaceful until they did something to bring about change.

In order to have peace in our own hearts, we must take a stand when something can be done so that we can live with integrity and purpose.

> Today I am going deep within me to find my strength.
> Today I am going deep within me to find the very best
> of me that I can offer to at least one other human being
> to make the world a better place to be.

I breathe softly into myself,
bringing awareness to any pain
I am feeling
at this moment.
I take this time now to stop and listen
to any emotional or physical
discomfort.
I pray that I do not act or speak
out of my own pain with the
intention of hurting someone else.

Man must evolve for all human conflict a method
which rejects revenge, aggression, and retaliation.
The foundation of such a method is love.
—Martin Luther King, Jr.

At some level, I know that every person in this entire world is my family. I am opening more and more to this realization and allowing myself to feel this connection deep within me.

I am holding my world family gently in my heart today.

I am sending thoughts of peace and love to my world family today.

Sitting quietly today, I am going deep within
my heart to find that place where we are all
connected . . . that place called love.

A Baha'i Prayer for Peace

Be generous in prosperity and thankful in adversity. Be fair in thy judgment and guarded in thy speech. Be a lamp unto those who walk in darkness and a home to the stranger. Be eyes to the blind and a guiding light unto the feet of the erring. Be a breath of life to the body of humankind, a dew to the soil of the human heart, and a fruit upon the tree of humility.

LOVE IS THICKER THAN CONCRETE
—*Painted on the Berlin Wall*
(from a picture taken by Terry Tillman)

We have tried everything but love. We have tried wars, torture, confinement, deprivation, restrictions, embargos, imprisonment, rules and regulations, discrimination, laws, and everything else.

Has the whole world ever tried love for just one day?

Today I will do my best to bring love to everything
I do, everyone I meet, and every thought I think.
I can feel the power of this thought as it is carried out
by all who are reading this page today!

I am just one of many meditating for world peace today.

I am just one of many making a contribution in the world today.

I am not less or more, but an important ONE

and that gives me a

great deal of peace and joy!

Human beings, by changing the inner attitudes of their minds,
can change the outer aspects of their lives.
—William James

Life is not always fair. People, places, and things do not always turn out the way we want them to or the way we think they should.

Sometimes we have to accept the truth, even when it is not to our liking.

Sometimes we have to just give up, let go, or give in to our powerlessness in order to find peace within ourselves.

Sometimes that is the only way peace is possible.

Today I release my control of outcomes and I experience
peace as I accept life on life's terms.

May there be peace within today.

May you trust your highest power that you are exactly where you are meant to be.

May you not forget the infinite possibilities that are born of faith.

May you use those gifts that you have received, and pass on the love that has been given to you.

May you be content knowing you are a child of God.

Let this presence settle into your bones, and allow your soul the freedom to sing, dance, praise, and love.

It is there for each and every one of you.

—Mother Teresa

*Holding on to anger, resentment, and hurt
only gives you tense muscles, a headache, and a sore jaw
from clenching your teeth. Forgiveness gives you back
the laughter and the lightness in your life.*
—Joan Lunden

Once we become aware that we create our own suffering, we would think it would be easy to let go of the things that make us suffer. But this is not always easy! Let's say, for example, that someone has stolen something we love. It might take a long time to forgive this person because of the pain this loss has caused us. Even though we know it is impossible to find peace when we are full of anger and resentment, it is also difficult at times to let them go.

But we can find ways once we are willing.

We can write a letter to express our feelings and then choose whether to mail it or not.

We can talk to a friend, family member, spiritual advisor, clergy, or therapist.

We can make amends if that is appropriate.

We can do a good deed.

We can pray and meditate.

We can ask for help and trust that help is on the way.

I am so grateful to know that willingness is just the beginning of a peaceful heart. There are so many things I can do once I have willingness.

Today is the first day of the rest of our lives.
—Author unknown

All of civilization has been on a journey that has brought us right here, right now, to this moment in time and space. Everything we did was necessary to get to where we are. We have come so far!

We are ready to take the next step on our spiritual journey, to experience and accept peace and freedom in our lives and to pass them on to others. We are participants in the spiritual transformation of civilization. Together we have the power to make it happen.

It is exciting to know that I am participating
in the spiritual transformation, first with myself
and then with all of civilization.

I am sending
peace
and
love
to everyone
on earth today.
This fills me
with
peace
and
love.

Fear knocked on the door.
Faith answered.
No one was there.

—Author unknown

When we have faith in a power greater than ourselves—when we know that, because of this faith, we are and will be okay no matter what happens—we have peace of mind. When things happen that make us fearful, we can go to this power, turn our fears over to it, and let go.

For some of us this faith comes easily. For others, it takes time. Be patient. The more you try this practice, the sooner you will experience a life that flows with greater ease and peace.

I am so grateful for the faith
I have in my Higher Power today!

A ZOROASTRIAN PRAYER FOR PEACE

We pray to God to eradicate all the misery in the world: that under-standing triumph over ignorance, that generosity triumph over indifference, that trust triumph over contempt, and that truth triumph over falsehood.

No if onlys, no what-ifs. . . just live . . . today!
—Jane Drury

One of the surest ways to guarantee a heavy heart is to look back at the past and wish it had been different. If only my husband, wife, mother, father, boss, or job had been different. What if I had been born rich? What if my spouse hadn't divorced me? What if I were beautiful or handsome or had more luck? If only I lived in a warmer, colder, rainier, drier climate. Then I would be happy today. Then I wouldn't be so depressed or lonely or poor or unlucky.

All the wishing in the world will not change the past, but this kind of thinking will pull you down, slow you down, and keep you stuck in your misery, giving you more of the same. It drains your energy and keeps you in a victim mode, blaming people and circumstances for any unhappiness. By placing the blame elsewhere, you fail to take responsibility for your life, and nothing will change.

Recognizing these patterns and being willing to change is your doorway to peace. Without if onlys and what-ifs, we become free to live in the joy of each moment.

*It is exciting to know that I am releasing
old patterns of thinking and opening the door
to joy and love and happiness and peace.*

My heart softens and expands
as I remember at least one thing
to be grateful for today.

There exists only the present instant . . . a Now which always
and without end is itself new. There is no yesterday nor any
tomorrow, but only Now, as it was a thousand years ago and
as it will be a thousand years hence.

—Meister Eckhart

We have everything we need right now. If we are fearful, we may be worried about the future. If we are angry or resentful, we are remembering the past. If we are stressed, we are reacting to what is going on in the present moment rather than flowing with it and accepting it.

If, instead, we stay in the present moment and feel our breath as it comes in and goes out, we can be at peace.

Stop now and

    feeeeeel

        the

           peace

              of the present instant.

I am at peace knowing I have everything
I need in the present moment.

People have a hard time letting go of their suffering. Out of a fear of the unknown, they prefer suffering that is familiar.
—Thich Nhat Hanh

The practice of "letting go" is so simple it is profound. Most of us cling to various familiar notions that cause our suffering. We believe things will not change. We think that we cannot change our habits. We trust that our loved ones will be with us forever. We even cling to the notion that using drugs, drinking alcohol, overeating, shopping, or gambling can make us happy. We believe that the way to happiness includes a quest for things like wealth, fame, power, and sex. If we look deeply at these notions, we will be able to see that this is not true and that we can choose to release them. Let's picture them as helium balloons on the ends of strings in our hands, then we can open our hands and let them float harmlessly up to the sky. Letting go of such things will reduce suffering and increase happiness.

Submitted by James W. Kershner

Today I recognize that I am clinging to notions that cause me suffering. I will practice letting go of these notions.

133

If we have no peace, it is because
we have forgotten we belong to each other.
—Mother Teresa

Many of us were brought up with the idea that our town, country, family, religion, color, or sexual preference is better than those of other people, and that our God is the only God. We have learned to take pride in our beliefs. This is accentuated when we are accepted into what we consider the "best" school, club, church, synagogue, or other group. We look down on others who belong to different groups or to none at all.

When did we forget that everyone is a child of God? That we all have opinions and beliefs, and that they are only opinions and beliefs, not facts? Inside of each of us beats a heart capable of accepting others, no matter how different they are from us.

Today I am looking at everyone as a child of God,
knowing that somewhere within each human being
is a heart and soul the same as mine.

Breathing in is my connection to God.

Breathing out is my awareness of the universe and all the people in it.

Breathing in, I pray that I can feel this connection to God all day long.

Breathing out, I pray that I can feel this connection to all human beings all day long.

The snowflakes fall, each flake in its appropriate place.
—Zen teaching

There is a higher order in the universe that is beyond our understanding.

We simply live with the results. Spring follows winter, which follows fall, which follows summer, and this happens year after year, century after century.

When we can turn our will and our lives over to the care of God—when we can trust that we are here for a purpose and then let go, knowing that we will know what we are to do when the time is right—then we will find peace. When we open ourselves to be a channel for Universal Energy to flow through us, we will always be inspired and strengthened.

I am trusting that my Higher Power is showing me exactly where I fit into my appropriate place in the world today. This fills me with great peace and joy.

A man is what he thinks about all day long.
—Ralph Waldo Emerson

I have found I can never get enough inspiration. No matter what kind of day I had yesterday, no matter what kind of sleep I had last night, I still need positive words that help connect me with God in the morning.

It's very helpful to read something spiritual or inspirational in the morning before praying and meditating. It helps to open our hearts and raise our awareness of God in our lives, and it keeps our thinking at a higher level of consciousness.

The more positive our day's beginning, the more positive our thinking and the happier and more peaceful we are throughout the day.

It feels so good to know that I am connected to God today. This creates love and peace and compassion and joy in my life.

Negative emotions corrode our connection to our Source.
—Author unknown

Negative emotions such as shame, guilt, anger, and resentment drain our energy. Negative emotions can block us from feeling joy and love, preventing God's creative energy from flowing through us, resulting in depression.

Today is a perfect day to watch what we think and how we respond to our thoughts. We can be aware of any negative thoughts and stop them before they become stories in our minds.

Take some time to examine whether you are holding on to any resentments, and write them down. Putting the words on paper helps to shine a light on them and make them clear. We can't deny what we see. The freedom that comes from being willing to examine and eliminate our negative emotions is a sure way to bring peace to our hearts.

It feels good to know that I am at choice today.
I can admit to any resentments I am holding
on to and become willing to let them go.

Today I turn to
a
power greater than myself
to guide me
on my
spiritual path
to peace,
leaving
the details
to
God.

They have healed also the hurt of the daughter of my people
slightly, saying, "Peace, peace," when there is no peace.
—Jeremiah 6:14

For us to have peace on Earth, we will first need to cultivate love, mutual respect, and understanding within our hearts. We will no longer be able to believe that this or that religion is the only way and that somehow only we are God's chosen ones and thus all others are somehow unclean or evil. Just as different nations have different languages, customs, and cultures, doesn't it follow that the people of those nations would likewise express their own innate divinity differently? After all, there is truth in all the world's great spiritual traditions.

If we can live according to the Golden Rule—doing unto others as we would have them do unto us—then we will create peace. If we could truly love one another, if everyone whose path crosses our own could be trusted, if everyone could be counted on to lend a helping hand, then this world would be a paradise. Let us strive to embody love, compassion, and peace in our lifetimes and share these qualities with others.

Let us not cry, Peace, peace, where there is no peace, or look to our governments and politicians to bring about peace in our world. Let us rather cultivate that peace and ineffable sweetness in each of our hearts and thereby be that peace in the world.

Submitted by Nigel J. Yorwerth, literary agent

It feels so good to go deep into my heart and be willing to let go of everything that is blocking me from finding peace.

The remarkable thing is that we really love our neighbor as ourselves: We do unto others as we do unto ourselves. We hate others when we hate ourselves. We are tolerant toward others when we tolerate ourselves. We forgive others when we forgive ourselves.
—Eric Hoffer

True peace will come when we release our prejudices, our biases, and embrace our humanness. We may talk of our desire for peace, but have we worked toward tolerance and acceptance in our words, in our actions, in our deeds? When we are in harmony with acceptance and love toward our fellow humans, then we will help create the essential elements needed for peace in our world.

Submitted by Joy Miller, PhD

Today I am aware that my inner peace is dependent on my tolerance for myself and others. I pray that I can be as accepting of others as I want everyone to be of me.

A knowledge of the path cannot be substituted
for putting one foot in front of the other.
—M.C. Richards

How often do we buy a book or read an article with a title that promises us instant success, like *5 Simple Secrets to Life, 12 Steps to Success*, or even *The Secret*, eagerly thinking, "This is it! I am going to get the answer to a happy or successful life . . . finally! I'll find the answer that others have known all along, the ones my parents failed to tell me. After all these years my life is going to become easier and I will be more successful!" How many times have you thought like this, only to discover, again and again, that nothing has really changed?

The truth is that nothing will change until we change. Reading and thinking are not going to help. Setting an intention, taking action steps, and changing our thoughts and our attitudes—these are the things that really are going to make a difference.

I trust I am being guided on my path to peace and love
today. I have everything I need to make my day one of
value to myself and those I meet along the way.

Meditation is not a way to enlightenment,
nor is it a method of achieving anything at all.
It is peace and blessedness in itself.
—Zen teaching

Meditation, simply being awake and aware in each moment, simply accepting what is in each moment, brings us peace. This is true whether we are sitting in formal meditation practice at a retreat or walking around in the supermarket or the garden. We can be mindful of the moment, be in the moment without thoughts, judgments, likes, or dislikes about the moment. Just be . . . in the moment.

We are connecting with our inner spirit. We are one with God. In the stillness, we can discover our blocks to inner peace and become willing to let them go.

I feel peace flowing through me as
I practice quieting my thinking mind.

It takes you only a minute to envision happiness, and your whole body will feel joyful. It will take only a minute to play the part of a wretched creature whom no one has befriended, and you will feel sorrow and pity for yourself.

—Ramtha

With just a few experiments, we can learn how powerful our thoughts are and how our thoughts create our feelings.

Take a few moments and remember a time when you felt embarrassed or ashamed as a child. Perhaps you gave the wrong answer at school. Perhaps you didn't get invited to a party or a dance. How do you feel as you remember this incident?

Now remember a time when you felt really good about yourself: a time when you accomplished something special or a time when you were rewarded or acknowledged for something you did. How do you feel as you remember this incident?

Now you see how you can change the way you feel by changing your thoughts—how you can choose to have peaceful, loving, and positive thoughts. This takes time and practice, but it is worth it.

Today I am letting go of all thoughts of self-doubt and inferiority and exchanging them for confident, loving, and peaceful thoughts.

We are not separate. Each of our actions, thoughts, and desires resonate in the Universe to be "picked up" by others.
—Marie T. Russell

What if everyone right now stopped and listened to their hearts, yes, stopped and listened to their hearts beat? Felt their rhythm? Felt their power?
We all have this same power keeping us alive.

Try it. Right now.

Breathe peace into the area where your heart lives.
Breathe peace out into the world.
Breathe love into the area where your heart lives.
Now breathe love out into the world.
Now feel that space where your heart lives stretch a little
  bigger to let more love in.
Breathe in love to fill that space.
Breathe in love to fill your entire body.
Breathe out love to fill our world.

I am bringing more awareness to my breath today, knowing I can change how I feel with just one breath as I breathe in thoughts of love and breathe love out into the world.

All Nature wears one universal grin.
—Tom Thumb the Great

There are times when I cannot find inner peace no matter how hard I try. Sometimes I feel anxious and irritable. Sometimes I feel frustrated or angry. It can happen on a working day, when there isn't enough time to do all that I want to do. But more often it happens on a day that I take off, when I'm trying to relax and I forget how.

When I feel negative or irritable moods that won't go away, I often go to the ocean, where I read or write or simply stare out at the waves. Sometimes I watch seagulls circle in the sky, dropping scallop shells on the sand, snacking on the meat as soon as the shells break open. My mind clears and I become one with the moment and there is nothing but peace.

Do you have a place where you can retreat to reconnect with yourself and your spirit? Is it the ocean, the forest, the mountains, or the desert? Perhaps it is taking a walk in the park or sitting under a favorite tree or simply being out of doors. Whatever it takes, it's important that we spend quiet time with nature and not let our dark moods stay unchanged.

When I am out of sorts, I can find some way to connect with nature to nurture my spirit and reconnect with my soul.

Always tell the truth. Then you'll never have to
remember what you said the last time.
—Sam Rayburn

One day, right before company was to arrive, I picked up a sponge from the corner of the bathtub, only to reveal a very dirty corner. My first impulse was to quickly move the sponge back to cover the dirt. I laughed at myself and took the few seconds to wipe the corner clean.

This made me think of how often we hide a bad motive under a good motive, trying to let people think we are doing something for them when all we really want is something for ourselves. We hide the truth in other ways too. When someone asks how we are, we say we're fine when we are really in turmoil or pain. Or we tell the part of a story that makes us look good. We certainly don't want to share our truth with others, especially when it is going to let them see us as less than we want to appear. And, of course, we even hide the truth from ourselves.

We find tremendous freedom and peace of mind when we don't have to worry about what story we told yesterday or what we are hiding under the sponge.

Today I am doing my best to be as honest as possible,
not only with others but with myself as well.

147

Tend all these shining things around you:
the smallest plant, the creatures and objects in your care.
Be gentle and nurture. Listen.

—Anne Hillman

Take a few moments to think of the word GENTLE.

What does it bring up for you?

The touch of a friend's hand?

Snowflakes slowly falling to the ground?

Holding a newborn puppy in your lap?

What other images come to mind when you think of the word GENTLE?

When you think the word GENTLE, what emotions do you feel?

Now breathe in the word GENTLE.

Let yourself feel peaceful and soft and sweet.

Today I am full of gentleness and I am
passing these feelings on to everyone I meet.

By the tender mercy of our God, the dawn from on high will
break upon us . . . to guide our feet into the way of peace.
—Luke 1:78-79

I see peace in the innocence of children's smiles when they are day-dreaming, in the eyes of lovers when they meet, and I feel my own personal peace in the early morning hours as dawn breaks and the presence of God reaches out to me.

I search for peace during those times when everything feels wrong and the sounds of quiet stir up thoughts that have invaded my peace of mind. It is then that I realize that not every moment of every day can always be quiet. Sometimes, too, peace can have its own music in the sound of people laughing together or a mother crying out as she gives birth to another of God's miracles, and oftentimes this kind of peace can warm my cold heart and gentle the turmoil in my head.

Submitted by Diane Crosby, Peace Corps volunteer

It is so comforting to know that I can change
a bad mood into a good mood when I am willing
to be inspired by people filled with joy and love.

A HINDU PRAYER FOR PEACE

Oh God, lead us from the unreal to the Real. Oh God, lead us from darkness to light. Oh God, lead us from death to immortality. Shanti, Shanti, Shanti unto all. Oh Lord God almighty, may there be peace in celestial regions. May there be peace on earth. May the waters be appeasing. May herbs be wholesome, and may trees and plants bring peace to all. May all beneficent beings bring peace to us. May thy Vedic Law propagate peace all through the world. May all things be a source of peace to us. And may thy peace itself bestow peace on all, and may that peace come to me also.

How to be happy now? By making peace
with the present moment.

—Eckhart Tolle

When we become locked into our stories of what we think life should or shouldn't be, we suffer.

When we hold on to thoughts of how we want this moment to be different, we suffer.

When we choose not to let go of our anger, resentment, guilt, shame, fears, what-ifs and if onlys, should haves and could haves, blaming and complaining, we suffer.

All we need to do is make a decision, set an intention, to be here now, feeling just this moment. Not the past, not the future. This moment. Now.

And let go of everything and anything that is keeping us from being right here. Now.

Peace is the complete acceptance of the present moment.

I am so grateful to practice being in the present moment,
knowing I can come back to this place anytime and
every time I remember.

What is peace? Is it war? No. Is it strife? No. Is it lovely,
and gentle, and beautiful, and pleasant, and serene, and joyful?
O yes!

—Charles Dickens

In the mid-'60s my therapist asked me what I wanted out of life and I said, "Peace of mind." Now it has been a part of my life for decades. I don't even know when it happened. But the rare moments when it is missing make me very uncomfortable. Time and surrender of self-will became healers. In my opinion, many people want the same thing, but unfortunately, they want their own way first. That is why we have wars.

I realize that it took many levels of surrender, beginning with giving up my need to be unique and always right. Magic words for me became "Maybe you are right." And the world did not come to an end. Working with others, being mentored as well as mentoring others, gave me great satisfaction. Doing work that I loved gave me not only peace of mind but true love of self.

Learning deep breathing taught me to relax and let go. I also learned the difference between a demand and a request, as simple as a change in tone of voice and facial expression. Others became more relaxed around me. I was able to forgive myself for my humanness. Peace evolved.

Submitted by Jane Drury

There are many paths to peace of mind and
today I am finding the right one for me.

I am filled with awareness of my in breath.

I am filled with awareness of my out breath.

I am filled with peace.

TODAY'S PEACEFUL EXERCISE

Today I am bringing my full awareness to a daily routine.

I am taking time to do at least five minutes of very slow walking.

I am being mindful of every aspect of my walking.

I am aware of the touch of my foot as I place it on the ground, the sand, or the rug.

I am aware of the feelings in my legs and my feet.

I am aware of my balance or lack of balance.

I am aware of aromas around me.

I am aware of any sounds that I hear, such as planes or birds or waves or cars or other people.

I am aware of the sights I see, such as flowers or trees or furniture or pictures on the walls.

If thoughts take me away from my awareness, I simply notice them and return my attention to my walking. I can do this any time during the day wherever I am.

This quiets my mind and gives me great peace.

I am carrying this peace with me for the rest of the day.

Don't Just Do Something, Sit There
—Title of a book by Sylvia Boorstein

The turmoil in the world today presents a prime opportunity to exercise our abilities for personal serenity. We can begin by resisting images of war and destruction and by making peace with our own bodies. The winter before we bombed Baghdad, some hardy women in a handful of communities around the globe chose to take this idea literally. They stripped off their clothes and spelled out P-E-A-C-E with their naked bodies. But we can participate at other levels, too, fully clothed, as long as we are also fully aware.

Walking the path of peace means surrendering the defenses we've constructed around our bodies, minds, and emotions so that the flow of spirit can enter. How do we surrender? Breathe—this is inspiration at its most literal. And when we breathe together it becomes *conspiracy*. Trust—hold the energy of yes instead of no. Expand the heart in love. Ask for help with an open hand. Sing the sudden music of praise. Or (perhaps most radically) stop doing. Simply hold space and allow the cycles of nature to work their magic. When we allow ourselves to connect deeply with the earth and with all the beings, seen and unseen, who inhabit it, we can never be at a total loss, even when the world around us seems to be spinning out of control.

Submitted by Gina Ogden, author of The Heart and Soul of Sex

I am opening my heart to the earth
and sending peace with every breath.

Everything in the universe has a purpose. Indeed,
the invisible intelligence that flows through everything
in a purposeful fashion is also flowing through you.
—Wayne Dyer

An ephemerid is a mayfly. The adult lives for only one day. The magic lies in its innate knowledge that that one day, in early spring, will be the most beautiful, sunniest day imaginable for the renewal cycle.

The mayflies emerge together from lakes and ponds, harmoniously, in tune with the cosmos at the exact hour and minute of first light. They molt and display shiny, fragile wings dried by the sun, then fly, mate, and live their lives in a flurry of activity, together, in a dance of life. They don't have mouth parts or digestive tracts, so there is no way for them to take in sustenance to extend their lives. At the exact setting of the sun, the dance ends and they lie down together, on calm waters, and the relaxation of death releases fertilized eggs that waft down through the darkness, safe from predators, and wait in silence for another generation's day in the sun.

I am taking time today to express my deepest gratitude to the
God of my understanding for each day I am alive and for the
truly magnificent gifts we have been given.

I am expanding
my heart
and letting it
fill
with
love.
This gives me so much
joy
and
peace.

There is only one way to happiness and that is to cease worrying about things which are beyond the power of our will.
—Epictetus

Is it going to rain for the picnic?

What will she think of me if I say that?

And the deeper worries: Will my marriage last forever? Is my daughter going to be happy with her career choice? Will I be accepted by the people in my new town? Will my son survive this illness? Will drugs take over my loved one's life? Will I ever be able to straighten out my confusion and stop being afraid? How can I overcome the jealousy that is ruining my relationships?

Those are the kinds of questions we cannot answer by ourselves or by willpower. Their answers are beyond our control. The more we worry about them, the more upset, nervous, and tense we become and the more we suffer.

By turning our worries over to God and trusting that we will get the answers when we need them, we can relax. By having faith that if things do not turn out the way we want them to, we will have the strength to get through anything, we can find peace.

I am so grateful to know that I do not have to worry about everything that is beyond my control. I can relax with the faith that God gives me all the strength I need today.

It has been said of the world's history hitherto that might makes right. It is for us and for our time to reverse the maxim and to say that right makes might.
—Abraham Lincoln

It is always within our power to be mighty. When we look to gain power, we often look to the big corporations, the wealthy, the political elite. We can feel like helpless supplicants, like the Scarecrow facing the Wizard of Oz. Paying less attention to the man behind the curtain makes it easier to see the ruby slippers on our own feet. World events spiraling out of control? Grab a bag and pick up litter along a road. Invest your money so that it benefits you and others. Treat your neighbors with a little more integrity each day. Wobbling toward balance in our own circle, we set the world to rights.

Submitted by Mary Jane LaVigne, Minnesota state leader of the Department of Peace Campaign

Today I remember my own power for good. Today I honor my many good works. In my integrity lies my strength.

Though I do not believe that a plant will spring up where no seed has been, I have great faith in a seed. Convince me you have a seed there, and I am prepared to expect wonders.
—Henry David Thoreau

Every morning we can plant the seeds of peace in our minds and in our hearts. We can read inspirational messages on peace. We can pray and meditate on peace. And we can become willing to let go of everything we are holding on to that is blocking us from peace. As we go through the day, we can bring our awareness to our breath and breathe in peace, especially in times of stress or disappointment.

Gradually the seeds we have planted grow stronger and stronger. Soon we are able to pass them on to others so that they, too, will be able to recognize them and find peace with each breath they take.

I am so grateful for the seeds of peace growing in me today. I can feel them with every breath I take.

It feels

so

good

to know

that I am a part

of

a

worldwide

spiritual

awakening

full of people

sending

PEACE

out into the

world

every day.

Our personal attempts to live humanly in this world are never wasted. Choosing to cultivate love rather than anger may just be what it takes to save the planet from extinction.
—Pema Chödrön

Whenever we make a mistake, do or say something foolish, come in last in a race, or don't get what we worked hard for, we can learn to be gentle, loving, compassionate, and forgiving with ourselves. Rather than beat ourselves up with anger, judgments, and condemnation, we can practice acceptance and move forward, knowing we are doing the best we can. As we develop these habits towards ourselves, it becomes more natural to extend the same respect to others who upset us.

Rather than snapping back in anger when we feel wronged, we can step back, breathe, and if we can't find forgiveness in our hearts, at least we can say nothing. When there is a person whom we dislike, we can usually find at least one acceptable quality, no matter how small, on which we can focus. And if we can't find a single positive attribute, we can know that this person was once a small innocent baby and is still a child of God.

Today I am practicing the art of gentleness, treating myself and everyone else the way I would like to be treated.

Smiling is infectious; you catch it like the flu.
When someone smiled at me today, I started smiling too.
I passed around the corner and someone saw my grin.
When he smiled I realized I passed it on to him.
I thought about that smile and then I realized its worth.
A single smile, just like mine, could travel round the earth.
So, if you feel a smile begin, don't leave it undetected.
Let's start an epidemic quick, and get the world infected!

—A very wise soul

There is a calmness to a life lived in Gratitude, a quiet joy.
—Ralph H. Blum

We can learn to be happy right in this moment . . . now. Think about it. Perhaps life isn't going the way you would like it to go, but you know what? There will always be things over which we are powerless. And when we get the things we think we want now, there will always be more things that we want.

So let today be a day when you spend some time looking at what you already have. And instead of wanting more, accept what you have with gratitude. Realize what you have really is enough . . . for right now.

Today I am letting myself feel the peace in accepting all that I have with gratitude.

Peace I bequeath to you, my own peace I give to you,
a peace which the world cannot give, that is my gift to you.
—John 14:27

Each of us has a story, a truth that rests within our souls that is waiting to be told, unfinished business that awaits acceptance. When we dare to enter into our story and listen to its truth, we find that God is already present, waiting to embrace us in loving acceptance. Ahh, and then comes the peace, the peace we are promised through God's Holy Spirit that lives within each of us, guiding our souls to new life and hope in ourselves, God, and others.

Submitted by Rev. Marie David, MEd, Reiki master

It feels so freeing to go deep within me and
find my truth, knowing that God accepts me, all of me,
just as I am, and brings me the gift of peace.

Be on the lookout for symptoms of inner peace.
The hearts of a great many have already been exposed
to inner peace and it is possible that people everywhere could
come down with it in epidemic proportions. This can pose a
serious threat to what has, up to now, been a fairly stable
condition of conflict in the world.

—Saskia Davis

More and more people every day are growing spiritually. Where the vast majority used to think that we could solve conflicts only through war, people are now turning to prayer and meditation with greater frequency. People are learning that peace begins with each and every one of us and that when we are peaceful, we pass peace on to all those with whom we come in contact.

This results naturally in our being happier.

What a wonderful vision this quote brings to mind.

Today I am focusing only on things that bring me inner
peace. I'm passing this on to others with a smile, a kind
word, a generous deed, or simply a loving thought.

Within you right now is the power to do things you never dreamed possible. This power becomes available to you just as you can change your beliefs.

—Maxwell Maltz

Do you feel stuck in some part of your life you think you cannot change? Do you think you can never have something you really want? Some of us were brought up with a belief system that has no basis in reality, and we carry negative, self-defeating messages with us for years into our adulthood. "I'll never be smart enough," "I'll never be rich enough," and "I'm not good enough" are just a few of the mantras that hold us back and create barriers to success. Perhaps you think there will always be wars or poverty or hunger or pain and suffering.

It's time to cancel your negative beliefs and open yourself up to a new way of thinking: that all things are possible with God. Change to this new way of thinking every time you have a negative thought. As soon as the negative thought comes in, think the word STOP! Now change that thought to one that allows possibilities for change and pray for guidance and direction to be part of making that change happen.

You'll soon see your energy increase, your attitude improve, and your life become fuller and more satisfying.

I feel power pouring through me as I open myself up to new possibilities in my life and in the world.

No matter what is going on in your life today,
take some quiet time.
Even if you think you don't have any spare time,
take some quiet time.
Listen to the wonder of silence.
Be aware of the power of the earth
beneath your feet.
Feel the magnificence of the sky
above you.
Be mindful of your breath coming in
and going out.
Notice your chest as it rises and falls.
Be aware of your stomach as it fills and empties.
Feel
the
quiet.
Know
the
peace.

*Love, then, consists in this: not that we have loved God,
but that God has loved us.*

—1 John 4:10

I believe that until each of us lives with the conviction that we are loved without condition, we remain too afraid to experience peace. Instead we seek the distraction provided by turmoil. We live believing in false needs that have their source in fear and we seek to provide first for ourselves because we believe no one else will.

When we ask for and accept the conviction that God loves us without condition, that God provides all we ever need, when we look Love in the eye and see our own reflection, then we are safe enough to live in peace.

Fear is falsehood; Love is the truth. We are neither in control nor out of control. The reality is we are created in grace to share control, to be co-Creators with God.

Submitted by James F. David, MDiv

*I pray today to be convinced once and forever of God's
unconditional love. As I ask and accept in faith,
I live as a co-Creator and know God's peace.*

*I see every human being as having good and bad tendencies,
impulses to charity and impulses to selfishness,
the desire to be truthful and the desire to lie.*
—Harold S. Kushner

It is comforting to know that many wise people believe that we all have good and bad tendencies. Therefore, when we struggle with our own desires, we are not unique, we are normal. It is this struggle that can make us better human beings. It is what we do with our decisions about these desires that will bring us peace of mind or keep us up at night.

How do we really want to feel? Is this selfish or hurtful act worth the pain we may feel later? These are the questions that only we can answer for ourselves.

*Today I am taking time to carefully consider
the emotional outcome of my decisions so that
I can make my choices bring me inner peace.*

Life is too short for drama and petty things, so kiss slowly, laugh insanely, love truly, and forgive quickly.
—Author unknown

How many times have you thought that you could never forgive this one or that one? He doesn't deserve forgiveness, you would think. Look what she did to me or someone else!

Or perhaps we don't forgive ourselves. We carry our guilt and shame with us like heavy stones around our necks, pulling us down, preventing us from ever feeling genuinely happy.

Forgiveness is one of the hardest undertakings to understand. When we hold on to anger, resentments, and old grudges, we become hardened. We close our hearts. We put up barriers between ourselves and others. We block our ability to feel love.

Forgiveness is simply a letting go, not a holding on. It is an acceptance of whatever has happened. It is over. It is done. It is not condoning or accepting unacceptable behavior. It is just choosing not to hold on to it. The relief we feel when we open ourselves to forgiveness is worth the struggle with our ego for the willingness to forgive. Once we have put that heavy stone of resentment down, we can, with a sigh of relief, stand tall, breathe deeply and smoothly, and feel our heart expand with love.

There is such peace in knowing that I can ask my Higher Power for the willingness to let go of all my anger and resentments, and I am willing.

171

Today
I am taking time
to send positive,
peaceful,
and
loving energy
first to myself
and then
out
to
all
the
people
in the
world,
feeling deeply
connected
to
everyone
praying
for
world
peace.

Until he extends his circle of compassion to include all living things, man will not himself find peace.
—Albert Schweitzer

Today let's focus on compassion.

First, please take some time in this day to sit quietly. Meditate in any way that feels right to you. When you feel quiet and peaceful, focus on your heart and let that place stretch a little bigger to let more love in.

Now imagine a time of difficulty in your life, whether it was a long time ago or is happening right now. Feel compassion pouring into your body. Feel yourself filling with compassion with every breath that you take. Sit quietly with this feeling and let yourself feel the healing and peace that is taking place.

Now imagine someone in your life having a difficult time and send the feeling of compassion to that person. Now send that same feeling to all those suffering in the world, all those who need compassion to heal.

Now imagine all the people reading this page who are sending compassion out into the world. Countless people all filling their hearts with compassion and sending it out to all people suffering.

Today I am filled with the amazing power of compassion as it flows through my heart and heals my life.

Have patience with all things, but chiefly have patience
with yourself. Do not lose courage in considering your own
imperfections but instantly set about remedying them—
every day begin the task anew.

—Saint Francis de Sales

Standing in a long line in the supermarket, sitting in the waiting room while your car is being fixed, or waiting to hear the results of your biopsy can be a wonderful time to practice patience. We have a choice. We can think of the endless things we have to do. We can be filled with fear and worry about what will happen if the result of the test is bad news. We can tap our foot in frustration or, if we're in line, stare at the heads of the people before us, willing them to hurry.

Or we can practice patience. We can drop our story about how busy we are or how important we are. We can pray for our fear to be changed to faith. We can breathe in peace and breathe out tension and impatience.

I can choose peace today by using every opportunity
that occurs to practice patience. It feels so good to know
I am at choice.

"How do you get to Carnegie Hall?"
"Practice, practice, practice!"
—Unknown sage

Some people experience spiritual transformation in an instant. Bill Wilson, a founder of Alcoholics Anonymous, was one. In the hospital, in desperation, in a deep state of suffering, he prayed to God for relief from his alcoholism. He writes that he saw a white light and felt God's spirit fill his room. There are numerous other stories of people who have been transformed through prayer, meditation, and other practices.

For most of us, the struggle to change, to be better people, to let go of anger and resentments and all our other habits that keep us from feeling peace, takes time. A lifetime of habitual, fearful thinking, for example, can take what feels like an eternity to turn into trust. We can become discouraged, thinking we are not making progress fast enough.

To change how we think and respond differently to life begins with willingness to let it happen. We must let go of all that we do to create our stress and suffering. We must be able to become aware, stay in the present moment, watch how we respond, think, and act, and then let go. This takes practice, practice, and more practice! For every two steps forward there can be one step backward. Progress happens a day at a time, a moment at a time, a thought at a time.

God gives me all the patience I need to practice
living a life of peace and passing it on.

A burden shared is a burden cut in half.
—Author unknown

Some of us find it difficult to talk about what is really going on in our lives; to share our secrets, our fears, and especially our shame. Some people say they will take certain things to the grave with them, that they will never reveal this or that. The fear of really letting ourselves be seen can override any advantage we receive when we share our burdens.

Instead, we choose to keep things inside and let them fester. Ultimately, this can make us sick. Harboring secrets keeps us stuck. Worries become exaggerated and take over our thoughts, destroying our special moments, blocking our peace of mind.

Finding just one person we trust, with whom we can be vulnerable, can bring us so much freedom. What a great relief it is to be able to trust enough to talk about what is going on in our lives. Knotted stomach muscles relax and our breath flows more freely. Depression, headaches, and back pain can even disappear as we feel healthier, happier, and more peaceful.

Today I pray that I can trust one person in my life with whom I can be completely honest. I ask for the willingness to let go of any fears that keep me from being completely open with this person.

Ring the bells that still can ring
Forget your perfect offering
There is a crack in everything
That's how the light gets in.

—Leonard Cohen

We so want to be perfect that we quickly get upset with ourselves when we don't meet our impossible expectations. We mentally beat ourselves up when we lose our tempers, forget appointments, get low grades, or get into fender-benders. We call ourselves names, use should haves and if onlys, and promise ourselves we will do better next time. It won't happen again. We'll be more careful.

But it will happen again. Perhaps not the same situations, but other examples of our imperfection will appear. And unless we change our attitude and accept our humanness, we'll never find peace. It's time to embrace the fact that we are not saints and to be gentle, loving, and forgiving of ourselves just as we are. It's time to look at ourselves through the eyes of love and compassion.

Today I am practicing treating myself as my own best friend and giving myself all the love and acceptance I deserve.

Today I am sending
a protective light
to all living beings
so that we may all be

safe

and

free

from

harm.

How wonderful it is that nobody need wait a single moment
before starting to improve the world.

—Anne Frank

We don't have to wait until we turn a certain age or take another course or until the other party is elected. We don't have to wait until we know more, become more disciplined, or retire. We don't have to wait until we have more time, read another book, or become more inspired.

The right time is NOW.

Today I am taking an action step to do
something positive for world peace.

There is no trust more sacred than the one the world holds with children. There is no duty more important than ensuring that their rights are respected, that their welfare is protected, that their lives are free from fear and want, and that they grow up in peace.
—Kofi A. Annan, former secretary-general of the United Nations

If we want to live in a world that is just and peaceful, we need to focus more attention, time, and resources on the world's children. They are our future. If we adults want to rid the world of war, we need to teach our children compromise and cooperation. We need to show respect for all people, old and young, rich and poor, male and female, black, white, brown, and red.

Children who live in extreme poverty, who lack homes to call their own, who worry each day about where they will get their next meal, who are being exploited and abused, who lack educational opportunities and are too tired to dream—we need to embrace these children and change their lives. They need to be nurtured, cared for, listened to, protected, and heard. Children are the leaders of tomorrow. Today we are the leaders of change. They are watching us. Let's show them how to be the grown-ups we wish them to be.

Today I can make a difference in the life of one child. I can hug a child just because; I can volunteer my time and talents; I can do any of a number of things to help children.

Submitted by Amy Shore, author, teacher, and adoption advocate

Today I am being the grown-up that I wish a child to be tomorrow . . . and this, today, in its own small way, can change the world for the better.

Be serene in the oneness of things and erroneous views
will disappear by themselves.

—Seng-ts'an

I love the above quote. It has the immediate effect of quieting my mind.

A quiet, still mind is more open, more receptive to the beauties and mysteries of life. It does begin to touch "the oneness of all things."

What happens when we touch this oneness? All our misconceptions resolve themselves. Success is guaranteed. This does not mean that we do not need to take action. It only points the way to where we must begin. Go first to the oneness of all things, and clarity and life-supporting action come forward.

Submitted by David A. Cronin, bookstore owner

Today I commit to five minutes of resting, as best I am able,
in this oneness. In this quietness of my mind I ask for
support from Spirit. Afterward, I will arise and move
throughout my day as I am guided and inspired.

On three things does the world exist:
on Torah, on worship, and on loving deeds.
—Simon the Righteous

Life goes from day to day with new discoveries and challenges, joys and sorrows, strife and peace. It is wonderful when we can look back and feel good about having made a difference, whether it be large or small, that made the world in some way better. And if we continue to have a goal for the future, the world will change still more.

So sit back, take a deep breath, and focus on the tasks you have as your goals in life. The three goals above that were written almost two thousand years ago are a good place to start. Following those goals may help you as you continue your journey on the road that leads to peace.

Submitted by Cantor Bruce Malin

I know I can make a difference in the world today
as I make an intention to learn more, to be thankful
for my gifts, and to give to others.

I am taking time
right now to

STOP

BREATHE

feel my breath
flow into my heart
and
feel
the
peace

and now I am
sending this peace
out
into
the
world.

All our dreams can come true if we
have the courage to pursue them.
—Walt Disney

It may take more courage than we think we have to interact with someone who is angry or fearful or hopeless. However, there is great courage in simply reaching out a hand to him or her in peace, bringing comfort where we know it is needed. With that simple act, ease replaces stress, and the world is made more peaceful in a way that can be repeated again and again, across borders and among diverse peoples.

Submitted by Sandy Bierig

Today, I will offer my hand and my willingness to bring peace to someone in need of it in the hope that my gesture will be repeated many times among people I will never know personally but with whom I will have had a deep connection.

*If we were to make a list of the people we don't like . . . we would
find out a lot about those aspects of ourselves that we can't face.*
—Pema Chödrön

One day many years ago, I looked at my dirty sneakers for the last time
and decided to finally wash them. Later, with my bright, white clean
sneakers, I attended a meeting. I noticed a man's dirty sneakers and
actually thought: "How could he wear such dirty sneakers?" It instantly
hit me that my sneakers had been just that dirty the day before, and I
saw how very judgmental I could be as I judged my judgmentalness.

Another time a friend asked me to name the five things I disliked about
someone. Easy! Then she asked if I had any of those traits. No, I answered.
Look deeply, she advised. Sure enough, I had to admit I had them all.

We can be angry at someone for being angry at us, irritated by
someone's irritability, impatient at someone's impatience.

Here's a wonderful exercise for today. Be mindful of how you
respond to any form of behavior that bothers you. Be honest and
examine yourself carefully, and admit it when you have the same habits
or characteristics.

As you make your discoveries, do so with gentleness and compassion
for yourself, not with judgment, shame, or criticism. Just shining a light
on your humanness is the beginning of your ability to change, to become
more loving and accepting of others, and to be a more compassionate
and peaceful person.

*Today I am feeling the freedom of gently allowing
myself to see and accept my imperfections.*

Today I am sending
prayers
to all
world leaders
so they
see
that
war
brings only
suffering.

PEACE
is the
answer.

Peace is not a goal, it is a practice.
—Thich Nhat Hanh

The idea of world peace is too big for me. So I think of peace in my world. I used to think that I could only have peace if certain external conditions were right. If only I had enough money. If only all my chores were done. If only my partner loved me enough. If only my car didn't break down. If only I were healthier. If only people were nicer to each other. If only, if only, if only. Of course the conditions were never all set, so there was no peace. When I took responsibility for becoming peace, this began to change.

Peace is available in the here and now, but we must learn how to help it materialize. It is not passive. It is not something we wait to have happen to us. It is something we practice. Once we realize this, we no longer blame the lack of peace on someone or something outside of us and we experience more peace. If we all took responsibility for our own peace, the world would be more peaceful.

Submitted by Jeff Eagle

It fills me with power and joy to know that I am responsible for peace in my life. I am practicing peace today!

Be pleasant until 10 o'clock in the morning and
the rest of the day will take care of itself.
—Elbert Hubbard

Often when we wake up, our minds are already going at full speed, planning all we have to do for the day or worrying about things that are coming up. We can be exhausted before even getting out of bed.

When we begin our mornings with inspirational readings, prayer, and meditation, it is amazing how different we feel. It's like putting into motion an intention for peace by knowing we are connected to God. Everything usually goes more smoothly because we have tuned in to a spiritual energy that we can recharge at any time during the day.

What a wonderful feeling it is to know that I can begin
each day with a practice that brings me peace.

We're only as sick as our secrets.
—Unknown sage

Many of us hold things inside that we vow we'll take to our grave. At first we don't realize that this sets up barriers between us and the people around us. We don't know that these secrets block us from being free, from feeling love, from living to our fullest potential.

Once we are willing to take a risk and share our secrets with just one other person, we can feel immense relief. It's as if we have been living in a very dark room, and we let the door open a crack by sharing with someone. And a speck of light shines in. Then, little by little, the door opens wider and wider and more light shines in, and pretty soon the room is flooded with light and we are free.

God is helping me let go of my fear of being seen for who I really am. Today I am taking that risk and am finding a person I can trust, with whom I can share at least one secret.

*The future belongs to those who believe
in the beauty of their dreams.*
—Eleanor Roosevelt

To dream of a world at peace, where everyone thinks of themselves as brothers and sisters in the human endeavor, is such a big image when taken as a whole. But when broken down into the communication of one person to another, then to another, and so on, it is possible. Certainly, it is a dream worth having and keeping safe and working toward steadily.

Submitted by Sandy Bierig

*Today, I will reach out to at least one other person
in peace and hope for our combined future.*

Just as I want to be happy,
may everyone be happy.

Just as I want to be peaceful,
may everyone be peaceful.

Just as I want to be safe,
may everyone be safe.

Just as I want to be free from suffering,
may everyone be free from suffering.

> When eating bamboo sprouts,
> remember the man who planted them.
> —Chinese proverb

So much that goes into everything we have in our lives is usually beyond our awareness. We wear clothes and eat food that we would not have, had not the toil of many people been involved long before these items reached our bodies and our tables.

By simply thinking of the planters, the pickers, the packers, and the shippers the next time you dress or eat, you can experience the interconnectedness of all human beings. What a wonderful, yet sad, feeling it is to be aware of our connections to each other. Wonderful in that we are all human beings with the same feelings and desires. Sad because the person planting our food might be underpaid and overworked, struggling to take care of his family, and maybe even living under the threat of war.

Stretching our mind with this awareness can help us remember how precious our lives are and remind us to treat every person with compassion and respect.

> Today I am opening my heart to people everywhere,
> knowing that we are all interconnected.

Gratitude is the memory of the heart.
—Jean-Baptiste Massieu

Gratitude is an amazing spirit lifter. No matter what mood you are in, no matter how low your mood is, the thought of just one thing for which you are grateful can lift your spirits. It doesn't even have to be something in your life right now. A pleasant memory or the thought of a good childhood friend can put an end to any negative mood. Or perhaps you'll think of a trip you are planning to take or a chance to visit your family.

Gratitude stimulates the feel-good hormones in your brain, letting them flow through your entire body, bringing instant results. Once you see how gratitude can transform your mood, you may want to make it a regular practice. There are so many blessings in our lives that we take for granted. Once we become mindful of gratitude, our list grows and grows.

Remember, you are in charge of what you feel in this moment. Choose gratitude!

Today I am willing to think about at least one thing for which I am grateful. I know gratitude can make any mood that I am in only better.

*I am a continually evolving being of light
and form amidst many others.*
—Author unknown

I really believe that peace is the joyful exchange of the body feeding the soul and the soul feeding the body. This is where we think reality into existence as our God-self, while enjoying the physicality of life as our human self. We are empowered to create our world, and we are humbled by our creations as they manifest.

Each person we meet is an opportunity to grow ourselves: to gain a deeper awareness, to share an amusing moment, to see a mirroring or expansion of ourselves. It is this gifting of ourselves and receiving of others that sustains and grows us.

Submitted by Rachel Hamill, founder of Wishing on a Star for Peace

---

*I am treating each person I meet today as a gift,
an opportunity, a chance to enrich and enjoy each other,
and this thought fills me with peace and joy.*

I must have decided wrongly because I am not at peace.
—A Course in Miracles

In any moment of any day, we can choose to feel peaceful. We can make a decision to give up our immediate, automatic reactions that bring us suffering and unhappiness. We can choose to give up our judgments, our anger, our fears, and our thoughts of revenge. We can choose to let go of our need to be right.

We can change our thoughts to love. We can turn our thoughts toward God.

It is a great comfort to know that I can choose to turn my thoughts to love and God and be peaceful, no matter what is going on in my life today.

We find comfort among those who agree with us,
growth among those who don't.

—Frank A. Clark

Notice how you feel the next time someone agrees with you or thinks you are right about something. Perhaps a feeling of pride comes up, or a feeling of self-satisfaction and comfort. There's nothing wrong with those feelings as long as you realize that they come from the outside. They are the result of our reaction to something that is said to us.

Notice how you feel the next time someone disagrees with you or thinks you are wrong. Perhaps a feeling of discomfort comes up. You might notice a tightening in your gut, a clenching of your fist or jaw. Perhaps you even hold your breath or snap back with a defensive retort. Be mindful of how you might want to defend your opinion or argue to change the other person's mind. There's nothing wrong with those feelings either, as long as you realize that they come from the outside. They are the result of our reaction to something that is said to us.

What a wonderful lesson in restraint, in pausing, in bringing our awareness to our breath and being quiet. When we let go of our need to be right, we can experience the peace of deep listening, of respecting another's point of view, of knowing there are many ways to look at any situation. We might even discover that our point of view is not the best one for us and that we can be open to learning from the opinion of others.

When I give up my need to be right, I am open to new ideas.
Today I am a student willing to learn from all who cross my path.

Today I am imagining everyone
on this planet
safe and free from harm.
With every out breath
I fill the world
with thoughts of
well-being
and
peace.

*In order to hear your calling and answer it, you must
generously give yourself the gift of time. It's not how fast you
make your dream come true, but how steadily you pursue it.*
—Sarah Ban Breathnach

The fact that world peace has not yet arrived is not something to feel discouraged about. If we consciously seek, we can spot signs all around us that peace is on the way. We can see that our dream, like fine aged wine, is growing richer with time. The impatience of youth must be allowed to mature. Just how noble is that for which we continue to dream; just how worthy is the quest? On this basis we can choose to dedicate ourselves to the pursuit of peace, knowing that someone somewhere will send up the final plea. Why not one of us?

Contributed by Nancy Jo Eckerson, founder of Write Now! Inc.

*I rededicate myself to the persevering spirit within me.
I pray for peace with renewed hope once more.
Not in my time, but in divine time, it shall come.*

I write about people who sometime in their life have a vision or dream of something that should be accomplished and they go to work. They are beaten over the head, knocked down, vilified, and for years they get nowhere. But every time they're knocked down they stand up. You cannot destroy these people. And at the end of their lives they've accomplished some modest part of what they set out to do.
—Irving Stone

Many of us might feel just like these characters who keep getting knocked down. We pray for peace, we work for peace, we march for peace, and yet the world still experiences wars and the threat of more wars. We might begin to think that our efforts and time are wasted.

It is important to know that each one of our individual efforts makes us stronger and more peaceful people, and that all the energy we are putting out into the world is being felt at a level we might not understand. In a 1974 experiment, scientists noted that in cities where one percent of the population had learned the technique of transcendental meditation, there was a decrease in the crime rate. At the same time, in matched control cities, the crime rate increased. More and more groups are forming all the time, adding more and more people to the peace movement. So while you might not be able to see immediate results, you can take a breath and feel peace in your heart, knowing that you are connected to an enormous movement for world peace.

It feels so powerful to know I am part of a planetary movement for peace, connected to countless people throughout the world.

To say you don't know is the beginning of knowing.
—Chinese proverb

Most of us have been brought up with certain ideas of what is right or wrong, good or bad. These beliefs come from our religion, our schools, our community, our nationality, or simply the ideas of our parents and their parents, and so on. So each of us has grown up thinking that what we have been taught is the truth, and we may go through a good part of our lives thinking that everyone else is wrong. We can be so full of what we think is true that we are not open to anything new—not even, perhaps, to the real truth!

This goes on until we receive the gift of awakening. Until we discover that there are two sides to every coin. Until we can be open to the realization that there are many ways of looking at the same thing, that there are many paths to the top of the mountain.

When we can wake up and be open to our need to be right, of thinking our belief is the only truth, our world opens up as the bud of a flower opens to become a beautiful blossom. A new world of understanding expands and our lives become so much richer.

*It is exciting to know that I can set aside all
that I believed as truth and become open to new ideas.
I am becoming wiser every day.*

If you know what is enough, you will have enough. But if you
wait until you have enough, you will never have enough.
—Confucius

What is enough for you? Do you have enough to eat? A place to sleep? Clothes to keep you warm? So often we think that if we had this or that, or more of this or that, we'd have enough. We'd be happy. If only we had a new car, but soon the new car will become old and we will want another new one. If only he or she loved us, but soon that person we want to love us might leave us—or have needs of his or her own to address. We might think one more drink or one more drug or just one more time will be enough. If we had one more, we would most likely want one *more!* It's a good thing to think about.

I am so grateful that I have all that I need today.
There is such peace and joy in knowing that when I accept
what I have with gratitude, I have enough of everything.

Any happiness and peace you experience, you bring to yourself through your attitude. Reframe your present by finding one thing to feel joy about right now.
—Sarah Ban Breathnach

Take some time today to sit quietly by yourself and
    give some thought to what brings you joy.
Does joy come from your family?
Friends?
Doing the work you love?
Being in nature?
What else brings you joy?
Sit here for as long as you want and let these feelings
    wash over you,
knowing that you can come back here at any time and
    bring them back.
Enjoy!

It gives me great peace to know that I can stop at any moment of the day and think of one thing that brings me joy, and that no matter what I was feeling before, it will change to joy.

*Help me, God, to understand that despite my best efforts to live
in peaceful serenity, there are times of mountain climbing.*
—Melody Beattie

No matter how hard we try, we are going to hit speed bumps on our spiritual path. We are human beings, not saints. We feel all emotions and all emotions are normal. There will be times of pain and sadness, anger and resentment, doubt and frustration.

It is in accepting our humanness that we can still find peace deep inside. Rather than holding on to these feelings, by accepting them we can allow them to pass.

*With God's help, I can still find peace, whatever
I am going through, whatever I am feeling.*

TODAY'S PEACEFUL EXERCISE

Today I am bringing my full awareness to a daily routine.

I am being mindful of every aspect of brushing my teeth.

I am aware of the touch of the water as it sprays into the sink.

I am aware of the sound of the water as it pours from the faucet.

I am aware of the smell of the toothpaste as I squeeze it onto my toothbrush.

I am aware of the taste of the toothpaste as I brush my teeth.

I am aware of the sight of the water and the toothpaste.

If thoughts take me away from my awareness, I simply take note of them and return my attention to this routine.

This quiets my mind and gives me great peace.

I am carrying this peace with me for the rest of the day.

Would that there were an award for people who come to
understand the concept of enough. Good enough. Successful enough.
Thin enough. Rich enough. Socially responsible enough.
When you have self-respect, you have enough.
                                                          —Gail Sheehy

How many times in one day do we judge ourselves, wanting to be better, do better, feel better? This lack of self-acceptance pulls us down, draining our energy, keeping us negative. It might not seem like it in the moment. We might even think we are being positive when we tell ourselves that next time we'll do better. There is a very subtle difference here. When we say this we are saying that this time is not good enough.

A slight shift in attitude toward acceptance can raise our energy level and even give us a sense of well-being. Rather than looking toward next time, be satisfied with right now.

If you trip on something, you just trip on something . . . no judgment. If you get angry, you just get angry. A normal emotion. No judgment. The more you practice acceptance, the more peaceful you will feel.

I am working on self-acceptance today. I am finding peace
in the knowledge that I am a good person getting better,
a child of God on a spiritual path.

When I come
from
my
heart,
my mind

slows

down
and
lets
go
of all
thoughts
that bring me
pain and
unhappiness.
Today
I choose
to come from
my
heart
and
feel
peace.

Let us love the world to peace.
—*Eileen Elias Freeman*

Centuries of saints, wise poets, and spiritual teachers have taught us that the only way to peace is through love. So why is our world still in such pain? Why do we still suffer?

Because we do not listen. Because there are powerful people among us who think war is an answer to peace. Some of our own leaders, the people we have chosen, believe in killing, in "wiping out" the enemy.

Yet more and more of us are beginning to understand the power of love, the power of oneness, and see that when we hurt another human being we are also hurting ourselves. And, as our numbers grow, our collective consciousness is a powerful force for change.

Today I am taking time to send loving thoughts out into the world. I know this is having a positive effect in ultimately bringing us all peace.

The greatest discovery of my generation is that a human being can alter his life by altering his attitudes of mind.
—William James

There are some days when it feels as if there is no way to have any peace. The washing machine might break down at the same time the bill collector calls for the third time, right after you've had a flat tire and are told it is not repairable, and through all this the dog won't stop barking. There are days when it seems that everything goes wrong. You wake up with a cold and the day only gets worse from there. And you think, "Why is everything happening to me?" There seems no end in sight.

However, peace can really be found, after all, in the acceptance of each moment, in the letting go of judging all that is happening as bad and in the putting aside the *poor mes*. So many difficult things don't usually happen on the same day, but difficult things do happen. Just simple acceptance, knowing that God is with you at all times, can bring many moments of peace through all the ups and downs of everyday life.

I can handle anything that comes up today as long as I remember that God is with me. I can find peace in the darkest moments through prayer and meditation.

No seed ever sees a flower.
—Zen teaching

Sometimes it feels as if we are making no progress at all. There are peace walks, peace gatherings, peace marches, peace prayers. Many of us try to elect politicians who believe in peace. Yet war continues to kill our children and destroy our countries.

We have no idea when our prayers will be heard or when the world will wake up to the healing powers of love, compassion, and acceptance.

We keep planting peace seeds and someday, whether it be seen by us, our children, or our children's children, there will be peace.

I find great peace in trusting that more and more people are planting seeds for peace and one day there will be a magnificent flowering around the world.

Whatever comes
up
today
that makes me feel
stressed,
agitated,
fearful, or
negative,
I can

STOP,

bring my awareness
to
my
breath,
and remember something
for which
I am grateful.
I can
feel
peace.

*Adapt yourself to the things among which your lot
has been cast and love sincerely the fellow creatures
with whom destiny has ordained that you shall live.*
—Marcus Aurelius

Most mothers and fathers begin to love their children as soon as they learn of their presence in the womb. Then they do everything they can to support and encourage the growth of the child. For a while, everything else is secondary to the new life process.

Continuing to love and care for their offspring, parents eventually return to their normal interest in other things such as careers, social interests, financial needs, and family responsibilities. Opinions and attitudes that were theirs all along reassert themselves, and life returns, more or less, to the state it was in before. I have heard people say things such as, "I like my own children, but I have difficulty around other people's." Love for one's own offspring does not necessarily expand to include the "fellow creatures" in our spheres. They remain different, separate from us, and not at all a part of what destiny has decreed we should share.

That is one reason why we can go to war, why we can gesture angrily to someone on the road who displeases us, why we can crowd out a neighbor at the store so we can be first in line. Thus, peace remains a distant ideal, desirable in concept but elusive in practice.

Submitted by Sandy Bierig

*Today, I will practice being open and kind to all I meet, thus moving
steadily toward the peace that I desire, which is a fine ideal.*

> *Blessed are the peacemakers,*
> *for they shall be called children of God.*
> —*Matthew 5:9*

One of my names for the Holy One is the Divine Disturber. For many years I have been disturbed, challenged, and supported in my prayers and efforts to be a peacemaker by this story:

An old rabbi once asked his pupils how they could tell when the night had ended and the day had begun.

"Could it be," asked one of the students, "when you can see an animal in the distance and tell whether it's a sheep or a dog?"

"No," answered the rabbi.

Another asked, "Is it when you can look at a tree in the distance and tell whether it's a fig tree or a peach tree?"

"No," answered the rabbi.

"Then when is it?" the pupils demanded.

"It is when you can look on the face of any man or woman and see that it is your sister or brother. Because if you cannot see this, it is still night."

Wanting to see the faces of humankind as my sisters and brothers and feeling called by Jesus to be a peacemaker, I embrace the practice of the Pause for Peace Initiative, a global grassroots campaign for peace and hope. Before my noon meal, I join thousands in affirming and praying: *I commit myself to peacemaking in a spirit of hope.*

Submitted by Sister Kay O'Neil, PBVM

I commit myself to peacemaking in a spirit of hope.

*The world only whispers her secrets to those who stand
still and listen. That's the reason the only difference
between "now" and "know" is one very silent letter.*
—Kate Nowak

Take some time today to sit quietly by yourself and give
some thought to the following:

First, what does PEACE really mean to you on a personal level?

Does it mean free from worries?

Getting along with everyone?

Being debt-free?

Having everything you need?

Having everything you want?

Being in nature?

Being close to God?

What else?

Now imagine how you would feel if you had this peace in
your heart.

Sit here for as long as you want and let these feelings of
peace wash over you.

Enjoy!

Today I am giving myself the gift of time and peace.

We create our lives a thought at a time. And sometimes, it comes down to changing a thought such as "Why did this happen to me?" into "There is a divine plan and there is a reason for this, and my choice is to create the most positive reaction I can."
—Dee Wallace Stone

Life sometimes gives us an unexpected disappointment, a jolt in our plans that can stop us in our tracks. Just when we're sure we are on the right path and will get where we need to be on time, the universe has a different idea. It might be as small as a red light or as large as a five-mile detour, a broken water pipe, or a flat tire that slows us down. It could even be a call for help from a friend or a sick child.

Whatever the case might be, we have a choice in how we handle the situation. We can create a long story about how unfair things can be or what bad luck we have. Or we can choose peace instead by choosing a positive reaction. We don't have to like the disappointment, but we can accept it with grace or we will suffer.

No matter what happens to my plans today, I trust that God is in charge.

We're always waiting for the perfect time. The perfect time doesn't arrive on a white stallion; it is generated as we face up to our challenges. Waiting only begets more waiting. Action begets action.
—Dawn Grove

Years ago, while trying to raise money for a halfway house for alcoholic women, I struggled to write a request for donations to local banks. I remember staying up night after night, crossing out lines, changing words, throwing away many pages of unacceptable letters. There came a point when I finally realized that if I waited for the perfect letter, we would never get the halfway house going. So I wrote the best letter I could and mailed it out to local banks. I then followed it up with a personal visit to each bank, and in no time enough donations came in so we could begin to help women to recover.

Perfection is most often a judgment in one's mind. Oh, we can do some things perfectly, such as finishing a crossword puzzle or following the ingredients in a recipe or passing an exam with all the right answers, but perfection in most things is a matter of personal opinion. Most often, if we wait to do something perfectly or wait for the perfect time, we miss out on many opportunities. We need to know that we are human beings, not gods or saints, and that we can only do the best we can in any given moment. It's only when we take chances that we will make things happen.

Today I trust that I am doing the best I can in any given moment and will go forward with my plans to achieve something new.

Right human relations is the only true peace.
—Alice A. Bailey

Throughout history, wise men and women have known that Alice was right. They have known that their only hope of peace in the world is to let go of striving to be better than others, to be more, to have more, to do more. It is the kind of trying that creates tension and prevents healthy, nonjudgmental interactions from happening between people. Watch children at play. They are relaxed together until one perceives that another has more toys and won't share them. Therein lie the seeds of war.

Submitted by Sandy Bierig

Today, I will seek to come from a place of peace in all my interactions with people.

True peace with oneself and with the world around us can only
be achieved through the development of mental peace.
—The Dalai Lama

In this mad technological world of overstimulation and overtalk, generating inner peace is an incredible challenge. I was fortunate to grow up very close to Mother Nature. I spent hours nestled in the woods by the Weir River relishing the stillness of a pine-needle bed hidden under the trees. It was quiet and calming. On the other end of town, we had a host of big caves. I could sit at the mouth of a cave for hours and just ponder. My sanctuaries were safe and beautiful. I could easily escape the traumas of childhood, go to my beloved hideaways, and get re-centered.

As an adult, I have learned to meditate and create the sounds of silence in my home. Lying still under a soft blanket and quieting my breathing helps me to reinstate inner peace and to connect me with the universe at large. I think we need to tune into our own inner wisdom and our own inner voice of truth and comfort. We can pray for ourselves and for world peace and for an end to suffering and the insanity of violence and politics.

My favorite getaway now is on a beach, where I can drive out and be alone with my thoughts. The glistening white sand between my toes helps release the tensions of the day. Being surrounded by water is as therapeutic as being embraced by my childhood forest. I need only to breathe out stress and inhale serenity and peacefulness to restore my tranquility.

Submitted by Gail McMeekin, author of The Power of Positive Choice

Today I am creating my own special place
where I can go and find inner peace.

*I love to think of nature as an unlimited broadcasting station,
through which God speaks to us every hour, if we will only tune in.*
—George Washington Carver

Here is an exercise that can truly add to your peace and serenity.

Sit in front of a tree or a plant outside or find one you can see from your window. If you do not have a tree or plant within sight, buy a plant today or have someone buy one for you. And if this is not possible, draw a picture of a tree or a plant.

Now sit where you can view this object and focus on it.

Breathe in and breathe out as you continue to give it your full awareness.

Contemplate the entire miracle of nature. Imagine the seed that began sprouting and growing until it grew into what is before you right now.

Now imagine millions and millions of seeds that grew into millions and millions of trees and plants in the world. Imagine you are sitting in the midst of all these wonders of nature, God's gifts to us.

Breathe in and breathe out. Feel yourself filling with peace with every breath.

Feel your entire body filling with peace.

Do this every day and watch your life change.

---

*It feels so good to know that I can be in nature
or simply see nature and find peace with every breath.*

With every in breath
I am filling with love.
With every out breath
I am letting go
of everything
that is blocking me
from feeling
love.

Filling.

Emptying.

*First keep the peace within yourself,
then you can also bring peace to others.*
—Thomas à Kempis

Take some time today just for you. Find a place where you won't be disturbed. Read the rest of this page through or, if you like, read the words out loud into a tape recorder so you can play them back. Then get comfortable and close your eyes.

Imagine yourself in a very beautiful place. Perhaps you remember a special place when you were on vacation. Perhaps you have a memory of a special place from childhood. Perhaps there is such a place in your life today. Or you can create a new place in your imagination. Imagine you are in this place. The sun is shining brightly. The weather is perfect.

Sit quietly in your special place. Know that no harm can come to you here. You are absolutely safe. Feel the warm sun on your body. There is a slight breeze gently blowing on your skin and hair.

Know that you can come back here anytime to relax and feel the peace.

Now feel your breath as it comes in and goes out.

With every in breath, know you are filling with peace.

With every out breath, know you are sending peace throughout the world.

Feel the peace.

*I am taking time today to find that special place
inside of me where peace lives.*

We must learn to reawaken and keep ourselves awake, not by mechanical aid, but by an infinite expectation of the dawn.
—Henry David Thoreau

There are some days in our lives when we just might feel like staying in bed and not facing the day. Life might appear boring or overwhelming or confusing or frightening. We can't seem to find the energy to do the simple things on our "to do" list, let alone go to work or school or anywhere else.

Rather than judging yourself at times like this, trust that it is only a mood and it will pass. Accept how you feel the same way you would notice the weather, without fear or judgment. The mood was created only by our thoughts, and thoughts are just thoughts. They are nothing more.

Nothing stays the same. Everything changes. Think of the mood as you would a cloudy day. The sun is still there but the clouds are blocking it from our view. Like the sun, our energy, our positive mood will return.

It's best to go through the day with only what must be done. Go through the motions. Pray. Meditate. Take one small action step at a time. And trust that this, too, shall pass.

I trust that no matter how I feel, God is with me, and I trust that I am getting through this day.

221

I have peace with me at all times.
—Spirithaven card

Many stores carry smooth flat stones with the word PEACE written or engraved on them. If you can't buy one, you can find a small smooth flat stone and write PEACE on it yourself. Then carry this stone with you in your pocket or purse or leave it on your desk or another place where you see it often.

In times of stress or upset, simply say to yourself:
I HAVE PEACE WITH ME AT ALL TIMES!
Feel the difference.
It works!

Today I know I can change how I feel in a moment by saying
I HAVE PEACE WITH ME AT ALL TIMES.
What a wonderful feeling!

How far to heaven? Just open your eyes and look.
You are in heaven.

—Sri Sri Ravi Shankar

Peace is our very nature. Peace is the one thing we all have in common. When I am overcome by anger or frustration, when someone hurts me or hurts others, and I want to react in that same hurtful way, it is in these times that I remember these are only feelings—and feelings are always changing. Today I may be laughing and tomorrow crying, one moment happy and the next angry or jealous. Feelings come and feelings go. I will be with these feelings, as we often have no choice, but I try not to let them rule me, define me, or linger unnecessarily.

When my head starts filling with regrets, worries, and fears, I stop and focus on my breath. Our breath is such a powerful tool to help silence our busy buzzing brains, and we can always count on it being there.

In silence we find our true selves, the ocean of peace that is constant and boundless within all of us. As we nourish this through meditation, all of the negativity begins to fade away. And just as the anger and rage of others can be contagious, so too is peace and love. So simply by being ourselves, each one of us has immense power to spread peace and heal this planet.

Submitted by Michael Collins, documentary filmmaker

I look forward to spending time in silence today
as I let all my tension and negativity fade away
and be replaced with love and peace.

What happens within us will create
what is happening outside of us.
—Dr. Joseph Dispenza

If we are filled with thoughts of fear or anger, we project those feelings out into our world, and the people around us are affected. If we are worried or depressed, the same is true. People are apt to respond to us in reaction to the feelings we are projecting.

When we expect to have bad things happen, they often do. When we see our world through negative eyes, there is a good chance we create a negative world.

By changing our attitudes and our thoughts, we can change our world.

I am being very careful today to do the best I can to express
outward thoughts of love, peace, and compassion.

Man stands in his own shadow and wonders why it is dark.
—Zen teaching

Imagine you are in a very dark room. Every time you move, you bump into something. You're sore and bruised but you are determined to get to the other side. Wouldn't it be easier and less painful to turn on the light? Then you can see what is in the room and make a clear path.

This is what meditation and prayer can do for us. We can discover what we are continually bumping into that is blocking us from getting to the other side—from following our spiritual path. Old habits, automatic ways of responding and reacting, are like the furniture that we keep bumping into and bruising ourselves on. Once we turn the light on in our interior room, we can see what is worth keeping and then ask God to help us remove everything else. Only then can we move forward on our spiritual path.

What freedom and peace there is in knowing that I can simply ask God to remove all that is blocking me on my spiritual path, and my journey will become clear.

JESUS' SERMON ON THE MOUNT
A CHRISTIAN PRAYER FOR PEACE

Blessed are the peacemakers, for they shall be known as the Children of God. But I say to you that hear, love your enemies, do good to those who hate you, bless those who curse you, pray for those who abuse you. To those who strike you on the cheek, offer the other also, and from those who take away your cloak, do not withhold your coat as well. Give to everyone who begs from you, and of those who take away your goods, do not ask them again. And as you wish that others would do to you, do so to them.

Replace heaviness and weariness of spirit with joy. Surround yourself with people and things that bring lightness of spirit.
—Melody Beattie

Choose to have fun today. Take time, even a small amount of time if that's all you can find, to do something you really enjoy.

Relax.

Let go.

Watch the stress and struggle fade away.

And when your fun time is over and it's time to get back to work or other everyday routines, choose not to pick up any problems or concerns or your long list of things to do. Leave them behind in the playground and simply choose to keep thoughts that maintain the fun and relaxed feeling.

Feel the peace.

No matter how busy I am today, I deserve to take time for fun. And I am doing just that!

For there lies peace, perfectly clear
because you have been willing to meet its conditions.
You can claim the Holy Instant anywhere you want it.
—A Course in Miracles

Whether allowing the paintbrush to gently glide across the water-soaked paper to create ribbons of luminous color, losing myself to a sacred chant, observing the tiny jade hummingbird do its dance among the bee balm, or laughing aloud while penning a silly children's poem—all are times where my spirit, in the Holy Instant, has found its true peace.

Moments released of any guilt, fear, resentment, or judgment—ego-free moments which often turn to hours, as time magically slips by unnoticed— are the blissful states that direct us straight to the heart of God.

Let's choose to follow a much gentler path. When we learn to give ourselves time away from our self-made world of noise, confusion, and illusion and instead surrender to God's leading, we then *become* that peace which we have for so long been seeking. The more our spirits are nurtured and peace-filled, the more likely we are to be reflections of that perfect peace for others in our world. We teach peace, we share peace, by being peace.

Submitted by Deb Bergstrom

Today I am stopping the search, the striving, the
FIGHTING for peace and remembering to take the time for
rest, for play, for nurturing myself, for going within to find
the bliss that will lead me straight to the heart of God.

A NATIVE AMERICAN PRAYER FOR PEACE

O Great Spirit of our Ancestors, I raise my pipe to you. To your messengers the four winds, and to Mother Earth who provides for your children. Give us the wisdom to teach our children to love, to respect, and to be kind to each other so that they may grow with peace in mind. Let us learn to share all the good things that you provide for us on this Earth.

It is in each of us that the peace of the world is cast . . .
in the frontiers of our hearts. From there, it must spread
out to the limits of the universe.

—Leon Joseph Cardinal Suenens

Many years ago I stood in a gift store in Poughkeepsie, New York, where this quote from Cardinal Suenens hung on a wall. I was captivated. For the first time in my young life, someone had actually articulated what I so deeply and personally believed: that peace outside of me, peace with all my relations, began with what I carried in my heart. If I couldn't generate peace there, I had no power to bring peace to bear outside of me. Not with the ones I loved intimately, nor strangers who might randomly cross my path, and most certainly not someone from another nation whose face I may never see and whose name I may never know.

Submitted by Meredith Jordan, founder of The Living Spiritual Elders Project

Each day I intentionally make the choice to live as if my one
life matters greatly to the presence of peace in our world.

*Meditation practice is regarded as a good and in fact
excellent way to overcome warfare in the world:
our own warfare as well as greater warfare.*
—Chögyam Trungpa Rinpoche

Somewhere deep inside we know that things can be better in this world. Somewhere deep inside there vibrates a frustration, a dissatisfaction with the way things are. Each time there is a war, no matter how far away, each and every one of us is affected at some level. Each time there is violence or crime or a child dies of starvation, we are affected. Something stirs within us and pushes us to take action. It is our choice whether or not we listen and act.

Many spiritual and religious organizations suggest the practice of meditation as a way of finding inner peace. Meditation has been taught for over twenty-six hundred years, so we can assume that it works. Meditation can be the action step that we take to heal our own pain and that of the world.

*I am filled with peace as I join with people everywhere
praying and meditating for peace. Today I am helping the
world move closer to peace by taking at least one action step.*

Now,
in this moment,
I am breathing in
all the positive,
loving,
and
peaceful
energies
of the
universe,
and as I
breathe
out,
I am sending them
to people everywhere.

Everything is flowing easily and effortlessly.
—Shakti Gawain

I read this quote many years ago and have said it to myself on countless occasions. It helped at times when I had to make an uncomfortable phone call or was waiting for a call from a doctor on test results. I have used it when a loan was due and while I waited for a grant for a project. Many other times over the years this quote has soothed me. It has taken away my fears and given me peace.

Thoughts like this have the power to change how we feel. It is amazing how quickly one word or phrase can work to shift us from a place of unhappiness to a place of joy, from a place of fear to a place of peace, from a place of anger to a place of compassion, from a place of resentment to a place of forgiveness. Use this quote or any other quote that works for you. Or make up your own.

Practice bringing your awareness to the thoughts that bring you stress and unhappiness. Watch how quickly those feelings change when you become willing to replace your thoughts with more spiritual and positive ones.

Today I am praying to slow down enough to watch my thoughts and change any unwanted ones to those that bring me peace.

Withdraw water from where weeds grow,
and they will wither; it's a natural law.

—Guy Finley

What an idea! If we don't nurture our negative thoughts, they can't last. If we stop ourselves every time we are aware of self-criticizing, judgmental, prejudicial, and fearful thoughts, they fade and end. If we are mindful when we are projecting into the future, or living in the past with anger or resentments, a space fills our mind and we can feel the peace of being in the now.

I am giving all my attention to positive,
loving, and peaceful thoughts today.

Everybody needs beauty as well as bread,
places to play in and pray in, where nature may heal
and give strength to body and soul alike.
—John Muir

Whether on a Saturday, a holy day, a birthday, or at the solstice, it is helpful to take the day off. And that means off from our jobs, from our housework, from our caring for others, from our busyness. We need to turn off the phone, the TV, the computer, the video games, and the MP3 player, put away the Sudoku, close our books, and get out of the house.

We need to be outdoors, if only in a quiet part of the park. We need to go to a pond, a river, or the ocean. To watch the tide come in and go out. To see clouds form up and drift away. To hear mourning doves, squirrels, the call of an occasional spiraling hawk. Feel the freshness of the air after rain, smell the rank riverbank at low water. Notice dewdrops resting on waterproof leaves or making fairy tablecloths on spider webs. See the varying colors on a plant's buds and its open and spent blossoms. Feel the giving ground of lawn and the solid strength of rock, and soak up the rising warmth of the climbing sun.

Our senses awaken; our hearts thump rhythmically, quietly. Our vision widens. Our sense of perspective is restored.

Submitted by Jo Chaffee

Peace is inevitable when a critical mass of us
maintain a balanced sense of perspective. Today I am
taking the time to restore my sense of beauty.

Many people have a wrong idea of what constitutes
true happiness. It is not attained through self-gratification,
but through fidelity to a worthy purpose.
—Helen Keller

One of the most important paths to inner peace is to find our soul's purpose. Until we have one, we feel a sense of incompleteness, as if something is missing from our lives. This may be so subtle it is barely felt at a conscious level. There might be an inner unrest, a longing for something unknown.

Each of us finds our own purpose in our own way. Some of us find it through pain and tragedy, for example, in recovering from addiction and then helping others do the same. Some of us find our purpose through prayer and meditation. Some are called into a religious order. Still others know what to do because they have a special skill or talent. Sometimes our purpose changes. What was true for twenty years can unexpectedly be transformed into a new path today.

It is in the development of an inner life that we can find our purpose. It is in silence, prayer, meditation, and being close to nature. It is in listening to and trusting our intuition, our inner voice, that we come to know what our next step is to help others, even if it is only one other person.

I am taking time today to go to my still,
quiet place within and listen for guidance.

If the only prayer you said in your whole life was
"thank you," that would suffice.
—Meister Eckhart

When I practice my spiritual program on a daily basis, I realize I do not become caught up in people, places, and things as much. My character defects do not flare up and make themselves known quite as often. Therefore, the inner freedom I've experienced as a result of practicing spiritual principles continues to grow. Gratitude is one of the key components that enable me to feel this freedom and a certain amount of peace.

Submitted by Kelly Warren

I have such a warm and peaceful feeling today
as I ask God to help me to always be mindful
of the gratitude I feel in my heart.

Now is the only time. How we relate to it creates the future.
In other words, if we're going to be more cheerful in the future,
it's because of our aspiration and exertion to be cheerful in
the present. What we do accumulates; the future is the result
of what we do right now.

—Pema Chödrön

Right now, right while you are reading these words, you can make your life peaceful. You do not have to take one step from where you are to change how you feel. You have the ability, the power, the gift from God to be peaceful right now.

By being aware of your breath as it comes in and goes out, you automatically slow down and stop your racing mind. So slow down. Stop. Notice your thoughts. You can, in this and every moment, notice the thoughts that create worry, stress, unhappiness, and the like, and choose to change those thoughts to peace, love, and compassion.

By doing this on a regular basis, you will soon see how you can create your own feelings by what you think. If you persist, you will, in time, do this automatically. Worry and other stressful thoughts will appear with less frequency and you will become a more peaceful person. And as a result, you will effortlessly send more peace out into the world.

It feels so good to know that whatever is going on in my life,
I can stop, be mindful of my breath, and feel peace.

People are often unreasonable, illogical, and self-centered.

Forgive them anyway.

If you are kind, people may accuse you of selfish, ulterior motives.

Be kind anyway.

If you are successful, you will win some false friends and some true enemies.

Succeed anyway.

If you are honest and frank, people may cheat you.

Be honest and frank anyway.

What you spend years building, someone could destroy overnight.

Build anyway.

If you find serenity and happiness, they may be jealous.

Be happy anyway.

The good you do today, people will often forget tomorrow.

Do good anyway.

Give the best you have, and it may never be enough.

Give the best you have anyway.

You see, in the final analysis, it is between you and God. It was never between you and them anyway.

—Mother Teresa

But oh! the blessing it is to have a friend to whom one can speak fearlessly on any subject; with whom one's deepest as well as one's most foolish thoughts come out simply and safely.
—Dinah Craik

Friendships are so important. Just to feel safe with another person can bring us comfort. In order to have any degree of inner peace, we need to be able to express what is going on within and not keep our worries, fears, resentments, and shame unexpressed.

We need someone in our lives with whom we can just be ourselves and share our hopes, our dreams, our deepest secrets. Someone we can not only call on when things are tough but with whom we can also share our victories.

It gives me great peace to know that I have someone I can talk to, no matter what is going on in my life.

> I learned that the interior of life was as rewarding
> as the exterior of life, and that my richest moments
> occurred when I was absolutely still.
>
> —Richard Bode

Research has shown that transformation is aided by deep listening in silence and stillness. It is so helpful to find some time to turn off all televisions, radios, phones, MP3 players, even dishwashers, and spend time in silence. You can pray, meditate, or contemplate. Simply be. Nothing more.

Going away to a retreat at least once a year is a wonderful way to experience silence. It may be more difficult at home, especially if you have young children. Wherever and however you can, it's good to make the space in your life for silence. Perhaps you can ask for help with it from a neighbor or a friend. You can even trade times when you help each other.

Silence feeds our soul, soothes our mind, heals our hearts. Silence transforms our world into one of peace.

I can find time today to be alone in silence.
Just this thought brings me peace.

In the world to come, I shall not be asked, "Why were you not Moses?" I shall be asked, "Why were you not Zusya?"
—Rabbi Zusya

When we are afraid of what others will think of us, or when we try to make an impression, we are acting, and this takes a great deal of energy and is very stressful. If we try to hide our fears and imperfections and act as if we have it all together, we are living a lie. If we act as if we know it all and that it is our way or no way, we will turn others away from us.

When we are simply ourselves, without any pretenses, life is so much more peaceful. When we are not trying to impress others, when we tell the truth about who we are, we can have a natural flow of communication with people. We don't have to live up to our own or anyone else's expectation of ourselves and we don't need to remember yesterday's lies.

The more we can accept ourselves exactly as we are, the easier it is to accept others exactly as they are. It is a joy to see how our relationship with ourselves and others improves as a result.

We can just be the imperfect, miraculous human beings that we are.

Today I am letting go of any shame that I am holding on to. I dare to let myself be seen just as I am, feeling the peace and wonder of simply being me.

May I be filled with peace.
May you be filled with peace.
May we all be filled with peace.

We are living through one of the most fundamental shifts in human history—a change in the actual belief structure in Western society. No economic, political, or military power can compare with the power of a change in the mind. By deliberately changing their images of reality, people are changing the world.
—Willis Hartman

Many say that we are in a new age of spiritual transformation. We are learning extensively about the nature of our minds and how we can use them to create inner and world peace. Scientists are making major breakthroughs each day in understanding the connection of mind, body, and spirit, affirming that our thoughts can create sickness or health, suffering or joy.

We are learning that we are not separate from each other and that when something happens to one of us, at some level it happens to all of us.

I am so grateful to learn that I can take responsibility for my feelings and fill my life and my world with peace, joy, and purpose.

Mankind must put an end to war, or war will put an end to mankind . . . War will exist until that distant day when the conscientious objector enjoys the same reputation and prestige that the warrior does today.
—John F. Kennedy

According to President Kennedy, ending war is in our own self-interest. How many irreplaceable people have been taken from the world in the name of satisfying the wants of aggressive people in all countries over centuries? Yet we go on destroying our youth and wasting our resources, endlessly. In recent times, we have seen young men in the United States take drastic measures to show their objection to war by burning draft cards, claiming conscientious objector status, leaving the country altogether, or marching to demonstrate how much they hate war. They have been called names and vilified at home and in the press, even though they felt that not demonstrating was immoral. After the Vietnam War, soldiers returning from fighting were not treated as heroes, but greeted with silence or angry chanting. Everybody suffered in such an atmosphere. Today, people try to show that they do not hate the veterans, just the war that maimed or took so many other young men forever. When will we learn, when will we ever learn?

Submitted by Sandy Bierig

Today I will follow the path of peace in all ways.

SEPTEMBER 2

It isn't enough to talk about peace. One must believe in it.
And it isn't enough to believe in it. One must work at it.
—Eleanor Roosevelt

Peace, like so many things in life, is not always what we think it is. Peace is not an absence of activity and it is not passivity, any more than it is walking away from our responsibilities to retreat to an island in the Pacific. Peace takes purposeful action, but from a center point that is open and receptive, for it knows that there is always more to know. When peace is at work within us, we trust deeply that what is at our door, or in our face, is exactly what we need right now. We ask plenty of questions and then leave enough space to listen for the answers. And we accept that what we hear may reveal a new place inside of us that we haven't known before.

While peace can step back to listen and learn, it's not afraid to step forward to speak. Peace can courageously take a stand for something or someone, but in a way that doesn't belittle anything or anyone. When we come from a place of peace, we don't have to make someone else wrong in order to affirm what is right for us. In short, peace is passionate, present, and therefore supremely powerful.

Submitted by Patricia Spadaro, writer

I listen quietly to my intuition and patiently wait for answers. When it is time for me to take an action step, I pray for courage, wisdom, and passion.

If you don't know what's meant by God,
watch a forsythia branch or a lettuce leaf sprout.
—Martin H. Fischer

It's not so much that God hears me personally when I pray; it's more like I am connecting with God. I have a deep knowing that God is everywhere and I can feel God's energy. When I pray to God for peace, something happens within me and I often feel peace.

Who or what is this God we pray to? Can we see God? Can we touch God? We don't really know God, except through faith.

The deeper our faith in a power greater than ourselves, the more connected we feel and the stronger is our source of strength.

I pray that my faith deepens and I turn more and more of
my life over to God, my source of strength and peace.

*Always repenting of wrongdoing will
never bring my heart to rest.*

—Chi K'ang

We will never have peace if we continually hold on to and beat ourselves up for the things we have done in the past. We need to make amends to those we have harmed, make restitution when appropriate, and, when we are able, forgive ourselves and then let go. Move on. It's this simple, if we are to live in the present moment and live in peace.

*Today I am doing all I can to express my sincere regrets to
anyone I have harmed, and then I am moving forward,
enjoying the peace and freedom of letting go.*

There is no recipe, no formula, no guidebook for self-care. We each have our own guide and that guide is within us. We need to ask the question: What do I need to do to take loving, responsible care of myself? Then we need to listen to the answer.
—Melody Beattie

Although it may seem selfish, our own needs must come first whenever possible. We can't effectively help anyone else if we are suffering from lack of self-care. We have to take time for ourselves each day to meditate, to pray, to just be. We have to talk about things that are bothering us so they won't fester inside. We must make sure we get enough rest and exercise and eat a healthy diet. We need to let go of any anger, resentment, guilt, and shame.

We don't need to do any of this perfectly. We simply need to practice taking care of ourselves, to nurture our mind, body, and soul in ways that work for us and bring us peace.

If we don't take care of ourselves, we'll have nothing to give to others, and we will be miserable.

It feels so good to take time for me today to do all I can to nurture my mind, body, and soul.

When the mind is not altered, it is clear.
When water is not disturbed, it is transparent.
—Mahamudra teaching

I was teaching a new meditation class recently in which four partici-pants had taken classes with me before and one person was new to the practice. I explained briefly about meditation for the new person, then asked the others to explain what I had missed. I wish I had recorded their comments because they were so wonderful—such an endorsement of and inspiration for meditation.

All four described wonderful changes that had occurred in their lives because of meditation. They said they were calmer and clearer and more peaceful. Relationships had improved for some. Work went better for others. They all felt better physically, mentally, and spiritually. It was a neon-sign advertisement for meditation.

I encourage everyone to meditate daily. The peace you will find is beyond words. And you will pass this peace on to others in your life.

No matter how busy I think I am,
I'm taking time to meditate today.

If you think you are too small to make an impact,
try going to bed with a mosquito in the room.
—Anita Roddick

Each of us has a unique and meaningful contribution to make to the world. It takes courage and inner strength to talk ourselves into claiming it. Sometimes courage is easy to come by because we are in the right place at the right time and we can say yes to the call of a force larger than ourselves.

Sometimes, though, we are deterred by restlessness, discontent, or depression. We know there is more, know there is a purpose for our lives, and know we are not living it.

Purpose unfolds when we answer the call to courage: when we speak our truth, regardless of consequences; when we move from what appears secure to make those choices that feel like a free fall into a bottomless pit. Those choices we make that excite us just as much as they scare us. However, it is in the places in between that we find out who we are and of what we are made.

What impact do you want to have in the world? What is the next step you can take in that direction? Not the big leap. Not the next ten steps. What is the next step? A beginning is all that is needed.

Submitted by Kathy L. Kidd, national field director, The Peace Alliance

I am free to choose the life I want to live.
I now take the next step in achieving my dream.

All we can do is try to rise beyond the question,
"Why did it happen?" and begin to ask the question,
"What do I do now that it has happened?"
—Harold S. Kushner

Certain trees are not predestined for destruction when hurricane-force winds rush through the forest. Trees fall at random. The same is true with tsunamis, earthquakes, and war. Trees fall and bombs explode. Innocent people die. It's not that some are chosen to die while others live. Life happens.

There is so much we do not understand and may never know. If we can accept that God has a larger plan and that the larger plan is for good and love, we can trust that while we are on this planet—even when everything feels hopeless—we are part of this plan. We can benefit by God's strength with every breath we take, even when we can't feel it. We can do the best we can.

Today I pray for the knowledge of God's will for me
and then follow my inner guidance. I choose to make
my thoughts and actions align with peace and love.

*Now, after years of observation and enough courage
to admit what I have observed, I try to plant peace if
I do not want discord; to plant loyalty and honesty
if I want to avoid betrayal and lies.*
—Maya Angelou

If we have resentments, we are holding on to anger. If we are being dishonest, whether or not we are consciously aware of it, fear creeps in as we are afraid of being caught in our lie. When we lack generosity, it is usually because we are fearful of not having enough. We cannot have a peaceful heart without spiritual values.

When we are aligned with spiritual principles such as loyalty, honesty, caring, compassion, generosity, and forgiveness, we feel peaceful. It is important that we make decisions that come from our hearts, decisions based on what is right for all concerned.

Sometimes those decisions are much harder to make, as they don't always give us what we want right now. For example, we might think cheating on a test will bring good marks and we will be happy. But what happens if we are caught? And the fear of being caught can bring us suffering. Integrity and inner peace are more important than immediate gratification.

*Today I pray for the wisdom, courage,
and strength to do what is right, knowing that
feeling good about myself brings inner peace.*

THE PRAYER OF ST. FRANCIS

Lord, make me an instrument of Thy peace;

Where there is hatred, let me sow love;

Where there is injury, pardon;

Where there is doubt, faith;

Where there is despair, hope;

Where there is darkness, light;

And where there is sadness, joy.

O Divine Master,

Grant that I may not so much seek to be consoled as to console;

To be understood, as to understand;

To be loved, as to love;

For it is in giving that we receive,

It is in pardoning that we are pardoned, and it is in dying

That we are born to Eternal Life.

Amen.

It's the action, not the fruit of the action, that's important. You have to do the right thing. It may not be in your power, may not be in your time, that there'll be any fruit. But that doesn't mean you stop doing the right thing. You may never know what results come from your action. But if you do nothing, there will be no result.
—Mahatma Gandhi

One day, while feeding our cat, Feather, I was about to give her a treat and chose not to. I didn't want her to expect a treat each time she was fed. Another time, as I was telling her "Good girl," I thought about giving her a treat and again thought better of it for the same reason. I do give her treats, but not always at the same time or for the same reasons.

This led my wandering mind to consider expectations. As the Buddha so wisely told us, when we have expectations, we suffer. We become disappointed. Yet, even knowing this, deep in my heart I have expectations for many things: that some day people will learn to live in peace, that everyone will have enough food, and that everyone will be happy. Is this something I expect to see in my lifetime? No, but it is out there as a goal.

What I know for sure is that I can do what I can today to make that goal a reality. I can pray. I can meditate. I can write books. I can send e-mails. Then I can leave the results to God. And like my cat, Feather, I won't have expectations for my treat right now, but someday it will be here.

When I have done all I can do today to bring peace to myself and the world, I will rest well, leaving the results to God.

As I
stop
today and
take the time to be still,
I get in touch with my Higher Power.
I feel myself filling with
love and
peace
as I relax
and let go
of the stress
in my
day,
and as I
stop
and
take this time for myself,
I pass
this
peace
on to others.

Nonviolence means avoiding not only external physical violence but also internal violence of spirit. You not only refuse to shoot a man, but you refuse to hate him.
—Martin Luther King, Jr.

It is not an easy thing to forgive someone for doing terrible things such as murder or rape. Anger and hate automatically loom up inside of us, as our natural survival instincts make us want to strike back in revenge.

It is much harder to let go of these feelings, which create violence in our own hearts. It takes a greater effort to realize that the perpetrators are human beings as well and suffer from their own anger, hatred, and other violent emotions.

The only way we can feel peace is to let go of our anger and hate. While this might seem like an impossible task, we can pray for the willingness to accomplish it. We can turn to a power greater than ourselves. First it might be a prayer for the willingness to be willing. And once we have made that intention, we will begin to experience peace. Our hearts will open and let more love in, and in time we will be able to let go of all that is blocking us from feeling peace.

Today I pray for the willingness to be willing to let go of all that is blocking my heart from feeling peace.

I object to violence because when it appears to do good, the good is only temporary; the evil it does is permanent.
—Mahatma Gandhi

There are many forms of violence other than war. There is the violence family members do to one another in an attempt to relieve their own suffering, such as calling a sibling a childhood name to get the upper hand in a dispute. Among grown-ups, this can embarrass and shame the person who is being ridiculed.

There is the violence of power that people exert over one another sometimes just because they can. We see this in contexts such as the workplace and in everyday transactions such as waiting to purchase something from a careless salesperson. Because I am a short, older person, I have waited in line at a convenience store watching the clerk serve all the people in front of me and then turn to some other task when it came my turn. Having had it happen several times, I know that is not my imagination. It is an act of ageism, and it is hurtful.

There is the careless parenting that allows children to be rude and disrespectful to others and fails to teach about kindness and consideration. There's the violence done to a marriage when one partner devalues the other or shows little care for his or her needs.

None of these are acts of war, but they do harm to others, and they work against peace.

Submitted by Sandy Bierig

Today I am aware of how I treat others in all of my interactions, both casual and significant.

The freedom to be human begins with the understanding that we need not act out all the inclinations arising within us.
—A. Olendski

How do you respond when someone doesn't agree with you?
How do you react when you don't get what you want?
What pushes your buttons enough to make you angry?
Have you ever felt such rage that you want to hurt someone?
Do you want to escape your reality in alcohol, drugs, sex, or food?

Think about these questions when you go through your day and realize that much of what you are feeling is felt by everyone at some level.

These feelings are somewhere deep within all of us—and sometimes, if we dare to admit it to ourselves, they are close to the surface. We have the same feelings our enemies have. As much as we would like to think of ourselves as kind, loving, and moral people—which is certainly our goal—we are not always that way.

There is a freedom in allowing ourselves to accept this truth. We are not saints. We are human beings, with all our wonderful good qualities and all our flaws. And as long as we learn that we do not have to react to these feelings, we can minimize our suffering.

I am learning to accept all my feelings as completely human. I practice refraining from reacting when I know my words and actions can hurt someone. I pray to come from a place of compassion and love.

The spiritual understanding of the individual is
the only understanding required for peace.
—Shirley MacLaine

There is no magical formula for finding inner peace. Nor is there one right way. For some of us, peace comes from a strong faith that God is always here to take care of us. For others, it might come from the belief that God is within and we will always know what to do. Some believe they have the inner strength to get through anything. Some find their path to peace in their religion. Others find it in spiritual communities or like-minded support groups. Many find inner peace through prayer, meditation, nature, or all of these.

Experiment. See what works for you. Talk to people you respect. Read inspirational books. Try various synagogues and churches and mosques. If your intention is to walk the path of inner peace, you will find yourself at the right door.

Today I am open to any and all direction
that guides me to inner peace.

Looking for peace is like looking for a turtle with a mustache:
You won't be able to find it. But when your heart is ready,
peace will come looking for you.
—Ajahn Chah

Inner peace comes from inner freedom. Locked-up anger, guilt, and shame keep us stuck in a world of suffering. A lifetime of repressed and suppressed thoughts about our unworthiness and faults keeps us stuck in torment and makes us physically, mentally, and spiritually sick.

It might take a counselor or therapist or member of the clergy to help us sort out the secrets from our past and loosen all the bonds that tie us to the past we are holding on to. We no longer have to live in shame and self-deprecation. Talking to a trusted person, expressing everything that is keeping us prisoner in unhappiness and turmoil, sets us on the road to freedom.

I pray for the willingness to be open and honest about anything I am holding within so I can be free to move forward. I pray for the willingness and courage to do everything it takes to find inner peace.

When I am disturbed, it is because I find some person, place, thing, or situation—some fact of my life—unacceptable to me, and I can find no serenity until I accept that person, place, thing, or situation as being exactly the way it is supposed to be at this moment.

—Alcoholics Anonymous Big Book

No matter how much we wish things were different from the way they are, they simply are not. They are what they are. We cannot change what is going on in the present moment. We can't change the person, place, thing, or situation. We can struggle. We can pray. We can complain. We can shout and beat our fists but we cannot change what is. Acceptance is all we can practice to maintain any peace.

It isn't always easy. We don't have to like it. We don't have to approve. We just have to say: "Yes, this is what is."

Praying helps. Turning the unwanted situation over to your Higher Power helps. Talking about it with a trusted friend helps. Journaling helps. But accept we must or all we will have instead is upset, frustration, anger, or suffering, and still nothing will change what is.

Peace comes with acceptance.

Today I am doing everything I can do to accept whatever is going on in each present moment.

We may never be strong enough to be entirely nonviolent in thought, word, and deed. But we must keep nonviolence as our goal and make strong progress towards it. The attainment of freedom, whether for a person, a nation, or a world, must be in exact proportion to the attainment of nonviolence for each.
—Mahatma Gandhi

How can we ever think about young men and women being killed and maimed in war and still have peace in our hearts? How can we hear about terrorists and suicide bombers and not feel rage?

We're not all like Mother Teresa, Jesus, Gandhi, or the Dalai Lama. Most of us can't just turn the other cheek. To have thoughts of anger and hatred is human under these circumstances, but we can choose not to act on our feelings. It is important that we not seek revenge or retaliate. To do so just perpetuates war and death and suffering. It is time for a new way of bringing peace to our world. It is time for communication whenever possible. It is time for both sides to really listen to each other. It is time for forgiveness and negotiation. It is time for prayer and meditation.

I pray that I may let go of destructive feelings about war and find peaceful ways I can contribute to ending violence.

Transformation is not so much a change in the person but a change in perspective. It is a profound shift in our human experience of consciousness that results in long-lasting alterations in worldview—how one experiences and relates to oneself, others, culture, nature, and the divine.
—*The Shift Report*

We all want to suffer less and enjoy life more. But how is this possible when things don't seem to be going our way?

Believe it or not, our minds are the answer. When we change our minds, we change our world. When we change our thoughts, our feelings change. Rather than looking at the glass as half empty, try looking at the glass as half full. Rather than seeing others as a threat or competition, or better or worse than you, or good or bad, or right or wrong, see them simply as human beings. Rather than beating yourself up because you are not who you would like to be, see yourself as a miracle, as a gift from God. Rather than being angry that it rained on your parade, be grateful that the rain is watering the flowers.

These suggestions might seem Pollyanna-ish, but they work! The more we can look at the bright side of things, the more joy we will have in our lives. The more we have thoughts of gratitude, compassion, and spirituality, the more we will have peace and love in our hearts. Transformation is a choice.

Today I am opening my heart to let more love in. I am being mindful of my thoughts and stopping any thought that does not come from my heart.

The energy of compassion in you will transform your life and make it more beautiful. Compassion is always born of understanding, and understanding is the result of looking deeply.

—Thich Nhat Hanh

When someone says or does something that brings up strong emotions in us, instead of reacting, we can go back to ourselves. We breathe, calm ourselves, and look deeply at the feeling that has come up in us in order to understand. Usually the feeling is not what we think it is. When we look deeply at what at first feels like anger, it may become clear that it is really covering hurt or sadness.

When we breathe with that feeling, sometimes a memory arises of another place, another time, when we had the same feeling. We can then send love and compassion to ourselves at that place and time. When we have taken care of ourselves in that way, we find that we can look at the person who we thought was the cause of our suffering in a new way. All we can see is his or her suffering. We feel nothing but compassion, and all we want to do is help that person suffer less.

I am so grateful that I can heal the past in the present moment, that I can untie the knots that are in me so that I can be free and at peace.

We deserve to be at peace with ourselves and others.
—*Melody Beattie*

Peace lies somewhere deep within all of us, often covered by pangs of shame and guilt over things we have done in the past or anger and resentment over things that have been done to us. To find that place of peace, we have to remove layer after layer of guilt and shame and anger and resentment.

We must come to a place of forgiveness, both for ourselves and for others.

First, we have to realize we are not perfect, we are only human, then forgive ourselves, making a commitment to do better in the future.

Where other people are involved, we have to make amends. We can never be free until we make restitution, apologize, and let go. At first this idea might be overwhelming. How can we put aside our pride and face up to our mistakes? It might take a simple prayer of asking God to give us the willingness, which can be the beginning of putting ourselves in the right frame of mind to make progress in this direction. Once we have the willingness, the next step—to speak directly to the person we have harmed—is easier. The freedom and peace we will feel will outweigh all the anxiety and resistance we once felt.

Submitted by Joanne Friday, meditation teacher

It feels so good to be willing to do all that I can to let go of all the layers that are blocking me from feeling inner peace.

We the peoples of the United Nations, determined to save succeeding generations from the scourge of war, which twice in our lifetime has brought untold sorrow to mankind, and to reaffirm faith in fundamental human rights, in the dignity and worth of the human person, in the equal rights of men and women and of nations large and small . . . and for these ends to practice tolerance and live together in peace with one another as good neighbors . . . have resolved to combine our efforts to accomplish these aims.

—Preamble to the charter of the United Nations

And Moses went and returned to Jethro his father-in-law, and said unto him, Let me go, I pray thee, and return unto my brethren that are in Egypt, and see whether they be yet alive. And Jethro said to Moses, Go in peace.

—Exodus 4:18

We are often reminded to "go in peace." But staying in peace during all the moments of the days is more difficult. Can I take this moment of peace, this place of peace, this breath of peace with me? How can I bring peace with me so that I stay in peace?

When we remember to return to our breath, whatever is going on in our lives, we can stay in peace, but it takes practice. The more we do it, the more we will remember to do it and the more it will become a habit.

Submitted by Tommie Ann Bower, interventionist

Today I am remembering the power of my breath and returning to it again and again, developing this as a habit to keep peace in my life.

Prayer, whether silent, chanted, or in meditation, is a way to return to ourselves in the present moment and touch the peace within us. It is, simultaneously, a way to put us in touch with the universal and the timeless.

—Thich Nhat Hanh

When we begin our day with prayer and meditation, everything seems to fall into place more easily. We know we are tuned in to a power greater than ourselves. We know we can turn to this power at all times during the day. We know that we are not in charge of the universe, that much of what happens during the day is out of our control, and that we can control only how we react to everything.

We can carry our problems as if they were a heavy burden, going over and over them, worrying about them, being pulled down by them, or we can let them go by turning them over to our Higher Power.

We can set an intention for peace, love, and compassion as we begin each day. We can be mindful of any negative thoughts and stop them as soon as they begin.

We can stop during the day and renew ourselves by bringing our awareness to our breath as we breathe in and out slowly three times. If anything disappointing happens, we can stop and repeat this process, connecting with God with every breath.

What a wonderful, comforting feeling it is to know that when I pray and meditate in the morning I have the best chance for having peace throughout the day. It is my choice.

If I told patients to raise their blood levels of immunoglobulins or killer T cells, no one would know how. But if I can teach them to love themselves and others fully, the same changes happen automatically.

—Bernie Siegel, MD

Scientists have known for some time that stress, anger, hate, resentment and other negative emotions raise blood pressure and shorten and speed breathing. These emotions affect many other parts of the body as well; they can even create disease. They hurt the person toward whom you feel those emotions, and they hurt you as well.

Feelings of love do just the opposite. Love reduces tension, decreases blood pressure, and lengthens and slows breathing. It is said that feelings of love can heal. They benefit both you and the receiver.

Love brings peace to us and others. Going into our hearts and consciously allowing love to come in can make the difference between a good day and a bad day. Sending out love to everyone fills us with peace while it heals our bodies. At the same time, it makes a difference to those around us.

When I send thoughts of love to myself, to my family and friends, and out into the world, I know I am making a difference. I know I am helping create world peace.

NOW
I am
breathing
in
love.
I am
breathing
in
health.
I am
breathing
in
peace.

Begin the day with love, spend the day with love, fill the day with love, end the day with love. That is the way to God.
—Swami Buaji

What happens when you first awaken in the morning? Are you aware of your first thoughts? Are they of worry and concern, of what you have to do during the day? Are they filled with your problems or are they filled with excitement and anticipation of the day ahead? Perhaps they immediately turn to God as you pray for guidance for this day.

As you begin this exercise, you might be surprised to find that you have formed habitual ways of thinking when you wake up. If you have tendencies to depression, you might wake up worried and uncomfortable or fearful. If you tend to be positive and optimistic, prospects for the day might excite you.

It is helpful to train yourself to bring your thoughts to the God of your understanding, turning your day over to your Higher Power and asking for guidance. Praying and meditating in the morning can help you stay connected to your source of peace, no matter what happens during the day.

I am filled with peace and love and comfort as I practice turning my thoughts to God when I wake up.

*Where is my faith? Even deep down . . . there is nothing but
emptiness and darkness . . . If there be God—please forgive me.*
—Mother Teresa

Most of us have periods in our lives that are dark and empty, times when we find ourselves in pain and turmoil, alone and confused. Perhaps we think that something is wrong with us, that we are being punished because of something we have done. Or maybe we think that there is no Higher Power after all, that God is merely an invention of some religion, a figment of someone's imagination. Some of us struggle to find a purpose. Others struggle to find God. Sometimes we feel close to God and other times far away.

It may help us to know that when we study the lives of saints, we discover that most of them had moments or periods in their lives when they faced doubt. They had painful, dark times when they didn't feel connected to God. They had times when they even doubted their purpose. They continued to pray and meditate, hoping to return to God and purpose.

When you go through times like this, know that you are not alone. Know that periods of darkness are almost always followed by a stronger faith, a deeper sense of peace, the strengthening of an old purpose, or the discovery of a new one. It helps to talk to someone on a spiritual path. It helps to write about it. It helps to pray and meditate. Above all, don't give up.

*No matter how I am feeling today, I am staying on my
spiritual path. I know that inner peace is possible when
I reach for a connection to a power greater than myself.
I can feel this peace right now in this present moment.*

Live today to the fullest because tomorrow is not promised.
—Author unknown

All we have is right now.

This breath.

This moment.

This time.

Now.

What you think and what you do in this moment pave the way
for your next moment. What you think and what you do in
this moment affect not only you but also your relationships
and, in some way, the world.

What do you want in this moment?

What can make your life full, peaceful, and meaningful?

This is a very precious moment. Use it wisely.

I pray that I make each moment of this day a moment
filled with healing and love and peace and purpose.

*Something as simple and natural as feeling and living
gratitude can be the essential spiritual ingredient for improving
any situation and lead to an overall happier, healthier life.*
—Chris Raymond

When you wake up in the morning and begin to become aware that you are awake, bring your mind to thoughts of gratitude. This is one of the surest ways to have a positive, peaceful day.

Before even getting out of bed, think of the things you have for which to be grateful. Think about family and friends. Think about the fact that you had a place to sleep and that soon you will be putting on clothes. Do you have water to wash in, gas in your car, a job to go to? Is there someone you love? Does someone love you? Even if you can come up with only one item, it can put peace in your heart and set the tone for a peaceful day.

*Today I am remembering everything I have
in my life for which to be grateful and this fills
me with a tremendous sense of peace.*

We cannot change our past. We cannot change the fact that people act in a certain way. We cannot change the inevitable. The only thing we can do is play on the one string we have, and that is our attitude.
—Charles Swindoll

There's a very simple method we can use to turn a bad mood around and change how we feel. It is called "replacing with the opposite." First, we have to be in touch with how we feel. Some feelings are easier to identify than others. If someone insults us, we may feel anger. If someone invites everyone else in the office to a party and leaves us out, there's a good chance we'll feel hurt. These feelings are easy to identify. Other feelings, such as boredom or dullness, might be harder to pin down. We might simply feel "blah" and not know exactly why.

This does not mean that we try to change appropriate feelings, such as sadness when we have experienced loss. We're talking about inappropriate feelings we hold on to, such as hate, revenge, anger, and fear.

First, let yourself feel any negative, unpleasant, or stressful feelings you have. Then decide whether you want to stay with them or not. If you are angry and know that this is doing you more harm than good, switch your thoughts to someone you love. If you are fearful, think about a person with whom you feel safe or a time when you felt very confident. Thoughts of the God of your understanding always help to change a feeling that's hurting you. Focusing on gratitude, compassion, and love can do wonders.

It is powerful to know that I can learn to make a choice to change how I think. Today I choose to think thoughts that bring me peace.

Have courage for the great sorrows of life and patience for the small ones; and when you have laboriously accomplished your daily task, go to sleep in peace. God is awake.
—Victor Hugo

When it is time for you to go to sleep, let go. Know you have done all you could do with this day. Let yourself feel good about your accomplishments. If you made any mistakes, they can be corrected tomorrow. Tomorrow is another day.

For now, rest well with the knowledge that there is nothing else you have to do. God is in charge of the universe and everything is in divine order.

---

*Tonight I rest in peace,
turning everything over to God.*

PAGAN PRAYER FOR CALM AND COMFORT

With your soothing fingers, wipe away the lines that worries have etched on our faces. Surround us with calm, let us rest in the glow of peace, as if we were encircled with the Moon's own light. Let our concerns and tensions drain away from us, pouring as water into your Earth.

—Ceisiwr Serith

I only went out for a walk and finally concluded to stay out
till sundown, for going out, I found, was really going in.
—John Muir

There are so many ways to walk. There is power walking and fast walking and competitive walking. There's walking for the purpose of getting somewhere and there's walking for the purpose of exercise. All walking is good for us physically and mentally.

Slow walking is good for us spiritually. It's wonderful to be able to take the time to look at and be with our surroundings. If we are lucky enough, we can notice the trees and the birds, the sky and the clouds, the earth, the flowers and weeds. If we are in a city filled with pavement and concrete streets and tall buildings, we can still be aware as we take each step, feeling the air fill our lungs, seeing the sky between buildings, and smiling at people as they pass us.

If it is impossible to get outside, we can take some time to walk around indoors, no matter how small our surroundings. Walking clears our heads, invigorates our bodies, and gives us a wonderful way to find some peace during a busy day.

No matter what is going on in my life today,
I will take at least a few moments to slow down and
feel the peace as I enjoy a walk.

Nothing that I can do will change the structure of the universe. But maybe by raising my voice I can help the greatest of all causes—goodwill among men and peace on earth.
—Albert Einstein

Most people think that their voice is too small and don't voice their discontent that could ripple.

Most people think their power is too limited and don't take a small action that could ripple.

Most people think their vision is too narrow and don't make a change that could ripple.

Most people think their reach is too short and don't grab a chance that could ripple.

Throw a pebble in the lake and see how far the ripples spread.

Voice your discontent.

Take small actions within your power.

Change what you see.

Grab what's in your reach.

Change can happen through the action of one person.

Change cannot happen through inaction.

Do what you believe is right, and watch the ripples spread.

Submitted by Judy Fishel, lawyer

It is a powerful feeling to know that my action step, combined with everyone else's, is helping to bring peace to our world.

TODAY'S PEACEFUL EXERCISE

Today I am bringing my full awareness to a daily routine.

I am being mindful of every aspect of going to bed.

I am aware of the touch of the water and the smell and taste of the toothpaste as I brush my teeth.

I am aware of the sound of the water as it pours from the faucet and the sight and smell of the soap as I wash my face.

I am aware of each piece of clothing and of how it feels against my skin as I take it off.

I am aware of what I do with each piece of clothing, whether I hang it up, put it in the laundry, or drop it on the floor.

I am aware of putting on my nightclothes and how they feel on my body.

I am aware of getting into bed, how the sheets feel against my skin, the pillow touching my head and my cheek.

I am aware of turning out the light and how it feels to be in the darkness.

I am aware of any thoughts or prayers I have when falling asleep.

If thoughts take me away from my awareness, I simply notice them and return my attention to my routine.

This quiets my mind and gives me great peace.

I am carrying this peace with me for the rest of the night.

Find your own quiet center of life,
and write from that to the world.
—Sarah Orne Jewett

Journaling is a wonderful technique to express ourselves, to pour out our heart and soul in a safe way. When we keep things inside, they fester and grow, destroying any chance for inner peace. Writing them down and talking about them is the doorway to freedom. One of the surest ways to block peace of mind is to hold on to all of our fear, anger, and resentment and not express it. When there is no one safe to speak to, or when we are alone, journaling is the best way to release this block to inner peace.

It's nice to buy a special notebook or journal, one that speaks to your heart, though this is not necessary. You might have a favorite pen you like to use. Don't worry about spelling, grammar, or punctuation. Just pour out all you are holding on to. Write down all thoughts that conjure up shame and embarrassment, any memory that makes you feel uncomfortable or guilty. Write about what is going on now in your life.

If you are concerned with someone reading your journal, write "Private and personal—please respect" on the front page. Hide it if necessary.

Journaling is freeing. You will be amazed at the relief it brings. Journaling can also be used as a daily practice. Just a few sentences beginning with "I feel . . ." can help you gain peace in your heart.

It feels so good to have a place where I can express myself safely.
I feel lighter and freer when I release all that I am feeling inside.

He that has light within his own clear breast
May sit i' th' center and enjoy bright day.
—John Milton

The first step toward a more peaceful world begins with a change of heart. It comes from honoring the light within our innermost being. As we consciously align ourselves with the energy of love that is deep inside us, we lighten and brighten our being, impacting everyone around us. It is then that we can shine our unique light on the world around us. True peace arises as you manifest the energy of your heart and soul.

Love is one of the strongest emotions we have, and the expression of love has a vibration or energy that lifts our spirits. Fear and worry, on the other hand, have a low energy that pulls us down. Open to the love inside and you will begin to see the universe in a different light. When we raise our vibrations, we can't help but raise the vibrations of those around us, creating peace in our own life as well.

Submitted by Janet Glass

I am love and I am light growing brighter
and brighter every day.

*The gap between what is and what should be is an ocean
of distress, disappointment, and frustrations.*
—Christina Feldman

Each time you feel a lack of peace, come quietly back to yourself. You might be surprised to discover that rather than accepting what is, you're either judging it or finding ways you think it should be different. If she would only be this way instead of that way. If he would only treat me this way instead of that way. The situation would be so much better if everyone did this instead of that.

Coming back gently to yourself, you can let go of everything you have been thinking. Coming back gently to yourself, you can slow your busy mind and find peace in the silence.

Peace lives in the silence.

*It's wonderful to know that I can let go of my judgments
when I return to the peaceful place that lies within me.
This is a gift and I am very grateful.*

Breathing in
I connect
with God.
Breathing out
I let go
of everything
that is blocking me
from
peace.
Breathing in
I turn over
all my blocks
to
God.
Breathing out
I
let
go.
Breathing in
I
let
God.

We have stopped for a moment to encounter each other.
To meet, to love, to share. It is a precious moment, but it is
transient. It is a little parenthesis in eternity. If we share with
caring, lightheartedness, and love, we will create abundance and
joy for each other, and this moment will have been worthwhile.
—Deepak Chopra, MD

Let's stop for a moment.

Breathe.

Bring your awareness to everyone reading this page today,
all for the same purpose: to bring peace to ourselves and
to the world.

What a wonderful thought!

What a wonderful intention!

What a wonderful moment!

I am filled with wonder and joy at the gift of my connection
to all people who are committed to world peace.

Please don't let my thoughts destroy my peace of mind.
—*Author unknown*

God Bags are wonderful to use when things are bothering you, when you are worried, when you feel stuck and when you can't let go. They're helpful when you are concerned about your own or someone else's health. They are good when you need to let go or when you want relief from pain, uncertainty, unhappiness. When you want to turn something over to God. When you finally come to the relief of knowing, "I can't. God can. I think I'll let God."

You can take any bag at all, plastic, paper, or cloth—or a box, if you prefer—and simply write GOD or HIGHER POWER on it, or write the name of the God of your understanding, or write nothing at all. You could even take a can and write GOD CAN! on it. You can do more, of course. You can paint or crayon a simple design or even embroider a fancy one. If this is not something you want others to see, be sure to put it in a safe place.

Then, when something is bothering you, write it down on a piece of paper, fold the paper, and put it in the bag, box, or can. When the worrisome thought recurs, say to yourself, "I have nothing to worry about. I have put it in the God Bag and God is handling it."

You will find this so freeing. It's a wonderful way to let go, let God, and have peace.

Whenever I have something that disturbs me that I can't resolve by myself, I am writing it down and turning it over to God. There's nothing more I need to do. It gives me so much peace to know that God is in charge.

*If we have the opportunity to be generous with our hearts,
ourselves, we have no idea of the depth and breadth of love's reach.*
—Margaret Cho

Generosity is such a wonderful gift. When we are generous to one
another, both the giver and the receiver feel good. Think about what you
can do to be generous today. Where can you help? Whom can you help?
It doesn't have to be anything big. Doing something small for the person
next door can help make the world a more peaceful place. We can drive
someone to the store or the doctor's office. We can shovel a driveway or
take in someone's paper.

We can read to the blind, volunteer at a hospital, be a big sister or a
big brother. There are always ways we can donate money. By keeping our
eyes and our hearts open, we can discover countless opportunities to
practice generosity. The list is endless.

Simply by making a decision to be more generous, you'll find your
heart begin to soften and your life begin to be filled with joy and peace.

*Today I am looking for ways I can be helpful.
Just this thought makes me feel good.*

Not by harming life
Does one become noble.
One is termed noble for being gentle
To all living things.

—Dhammapada

It is easy to be gentle with babies and puppies and cute little kittens. It is easy to be gentle with people we love. But all living things? The spider that is crawling on your ceiling? The man who steps on your toe at the supermarket? The woman who beats you to a parking space? Your enemies? Not so easy! And sometimes impossible.

We can experience how being the opposite of gentle—feeling angry, harsh, or brusque—makes us feel. Certainly not peaceful. Definitely not happy.

Rather than beating yourself up when you can't be gentle in thought or in action, why not make this an intention today and do the best you can toward this goal? Change happens slowly, but it doesn't happen at all until we desire it.

Today I pray for the willingness to be gentle to all living things so that I may have peace in my heart and pass it on.

It is not the road ahead that wears you out;
it is the grain of sand in your shoe.
—Arabic proverb

What keeps you up at night?

What are you afraid of letting anyone know about you?

Is there something you tell yourself you will take to the grave?

Is there someone you refuse to forgive?

Are there amends you need to make?

Is there a debt that goes unpaid?

If you answer yes to any one of these questions, you will not find inner peace, no matter where or how hard you look. It's time to think about what you are holding on to and pray for the willingness and guidance to do what needs to be done in order to be free.

If you answer no to these questions, you are doing good spiritual work. Congratulations. Enjoy your peace.

Today I am examining myself thoroughly and praying for the willingness and courage to do what I need to do for inner peace.

*Always remember that striving and struggle precede success,
even in the dictionary.*
—Sarah Ban Breathnach

There are times when we think we are doing everything that needs to be done to improve our life and the lives of those around us. We work hard and try to be helpful in our community. We do our best to stay positive, follow spiritual principles, and work for good causes. Yet our world is still in chaos and pain. Wars and violence continue. Rape, murder, and scandal are as common as the sun and the moon.

Hang in there. Everything takes time. Don't give up. Changes happen very slowly, yet they happen. Spiritual journeys are historically filled with detours into upset and disappointment. Look back over history and see how far we have come in regard to human rights. Look at the advances in medicine and other sciences. Even many religions are changing, albeit ever so slowly, to be more open and accepting. Trust that God has the answer and it is peace.

Let yourself have personal satisfaction in the effort you are making, even when the results aren't obvious.

*I pray that I may continue to have faith and patience
through the hardest times, knowing that dawn always
follows the darkest night.*

By a gradual falling of raindrops, a jar is filled.
However big the jar is, it is filled.
—Author unknown

At the time of this writing there are 5,710,000 world peace Web sites. Can you imagine the power we have to bring peace to the world with all this energy? Imagine combining the power of those people with the power of all the people reading this page today. Incredible power! Awesome energy! Peace is happening.

I can feel the power as I read this page.
The force that we are all creating is immense.
It feels so good to be connected to such
powerful energy for peace.

We are injured and hurt emotionally, not so much by other people or what they say and don't say, but by our own attitude and our own response.

—Maxwell Maltz

When someone hurts or upsets us, it's a natural reaction to want to hurt back, lash out, or punish the other person. This, of course, results in more upset and pain. When we hold on to these angry or hurt feelings, it takes much more of an effort not to respond and, if necessary, to walk away.

When we can create some space between our offender and ourselves, we can see how our upset comes from our own reaction to what has been said. Once we see this, we can realize that we have the ability to change how we react and thus change how we feel. What powerful knowledge this is, to know that we are in charge of our own feelings. We can respond with anger or we can choose not to respond at all. We can let go, knowing that what was said was just words, and not necessarily true words.

Today I am practicing breathing in peace and breathing out peace before I respond to anyone.

A Buddhist Prayer

May our heart's garden of awakening
   bloom with hundreds of flowers.
May we bring the feelings of peace and joy
   into every household.
May we plant wholesome seeds on ten
   thousand paths.
May we never attempt to escape the
   suffering of the world,
always being present when beings need
   our help.
May mountains and rivers be our witness
in this moment as we bow our heads and request
the Lord of Compassion
to embrace us all.

Sharing our fears in a loving manner
can deepen our intimate relationships.
—From a horoscope

One of the hardest things for some of us to do is to share our pain and struggles with others. Our ego says, "Don't let anyone see me. I want people to think I have it all together." So we stay bottled up, unaware that our unshared feelings keep us sick and block us from feeling peace in our hearts.

Let your heart open. Take a risk. Let someone else see you as you really are. Share your secret fears. You will find such a wonderful relief and your heart will be at peace.

I pray for the willingness to let go of my fears
by sharing them with a trusted friend.

Be still and know that I am God.

—Psalm 46:10

In order to maintain peace, follow God.

Walk the path of life, go where doors open, and recognize when the path closes.

Be flexible wherever God brings you, whether you like it or not.

Follow God's spirit wherever you go.

Submitted by Tom E. Largy

I am keeping my path simple and clear today so
I can be open to wherever God leads me.

Faith is fear that has said its prayers.
—*Author unknown*

Fear can be a lifesaver. It is a natural, God-given instinct that makes us act quickly when we are threatened. When we turn our fear over to the care of God, we are able to trust that we can handle the outcome. For instance, when a car turns the corner suddenly and speeds toward us, adrenaline flows quickly and we are given the strength to jump out of the way.

When fear comes from projecting our thoughts into the future, it is one of the biggest blocks to inner peace. What will happen if my child gets sick or I lose my job? What if a hurricane comes and destroys my house next year? What if I never find someone to love?

We can ask God to remove our unrealistic fears, and we can make a conscious effort to realize they are just thoughts. The peace of mind we will achieve when we change our habitual, fearful thinking is incredible.

When I become aware of fearful thoughts and feelings, I turn them over to my Higher Power. I am so grateful for the peace I feel as a result.

If you want others to be happy, practice compassion.
If you want to be happy, practice compassion.
—The Dalai Lama

Compassion can be defined as the ability to recognize suffering in others combined with a desire to alleviate it.

Think about the oppressed, the poor, the hungry, the sick. Think about people who have suffered so much because of war and natural disasters.

If we can open our hearts to their suffering, we can look for an area in which we can help to relieve suffering. We can choose one thing to do today to make the world a more peaceful place. If it is not possible to take an action step today, we can make taking such a step an intention for the future.

Today I pray for all people, for everyone suffering
in the world, that the power of all our accumulated prayers
may bring peace to the hearts of those who suffer.
I pray that our prayers may lead to the actions
necessary to make this happen.

It feels so good
to be
joined together
with so many people
in the power
and
energy
of prayer
to end suffering
in
the world.

> *Positive and negative are directions.*
> *Which direction do you choose?*
>
> —*Remez Sasson*

Negative thinking is such a burden. It is so heavy it pulls us down, draining our energy. Think about the difference between these two thoughts:

1. I have so much to do I'll never get it done.
2. I have all the time I need to accomplish today's goals.

The first is obviously depressing, depleting our spirits. It's not possible to feel peaceful when we are negative. The second is a spirit lifter.

Take time today to be aware of your thoughts. Every time you become aware of a negative thought, turn it into a positive thought. You will feel the difference immediately. Often we struggle against changing a negative thought, thinking that the positive one isn't true. This is where "act as if" comes in, helping us convert our old, dreary habitual thinking into spirit-lifting joy and peace.

Not only will you feel better and accomplish more, but the people around you will feel better in your presence. A small switch in your thinking can help lift the mood of everyone today.

Today I am mindful of all of my thoughts, converting any negative thoughts into positive ones. I am watching my mood and energy change as I feel more positive and peaceful about myself and my life.

*Self-pity is one of the most unhappy and consuming defects
that we know. It is a bar to all spiritual progress and can
cut off all effective communication with our fellows because of
its inordinate demands for attention and sympathy. It is a
maudlin form of martyrdom, which we can ill afford.*
—Bill Wilson

There's an old saying that one should take no more than fifteen minutes for self-pity a day and that's all. Self-pity pulls us deep into the dark side of ourselves. It pulls us down with its negativity and heavy self-indulgence. It keeps the focus outside of ourselves and blames persons, places, and things for our unhappiness, disappointments, and failures. It prevents us from taking responsibility for our own lives.

Whenever you find yourself in the throes of self-pity, it's best to stop it right away. Pray for it to be removed as quickly as possible before it leads to depression. Then look within yourself for reasons why your life is as it is. Remember, you have the power to make your life better and more peaceful. No one else can do that for you.

*I pray that I can see myself as clearly and honestly as possible.
I pray that God is helping me take responsibility for my own life
so that I can grow spiritually and find peace in my heart.*

If faith were rational, it wouldn't be—by definition—faith.
Faith is what you cannot see or prove or touch. Faith is
walking face-first and full speed into the dark. If we truly knew
all the answers in advance as to the meaning of life and the
nature of God and the destiny of our souls, our belief would not
be a leap of faith and it would not be a courageous act of
humanity; it would just be . . . a prudent insurance policy.
—Elizabeth Gilbert

Some of us live all our lives with our childhood understanding of God. Others challenge what they were taught as they grow older, question God and religion, and perhaps become agnostics or atheists. Eventually many begin their own personal journey by reading, attending various religious and spiritual services, studying with different teachers, and trying to find their own answers, their own God.

Some people pray even if they don't believe in God. They pray "just in case." For those of us who do pray, sometimes we pray and nothing happens, at least on the surface. But, just often enough, our prayers are answered and we begin to develop faith that there is a Power on which we can rely.

We come to believe that this Power can bring peace to the world through the power of prayer and right action. Our blind faith joins with countless others who have blind faith and we make it happen, one day at a time.

Deep in my heart and soul I know that God wants peace in
the world and I am doing what I can do to make it happen.

*Accustomed long to contemplating love and compassion,
I have forgotten all differences between myself and others.*
—Milarepa

If we are ever to have peace in our own hearts and peace in the world, we have to cultivate compassion. We must let go of the fears and anger and resistance that keep us in a world so quick to fight and kill.

We can begin practicing compassion for ourselves. Every time we think of something that brings us guilt or shame, we can forgive ourselves. Every time we make a mistake, we can treat ourselves with compassion and without blame. Every time we do something that we think we could have done better, we can accept ourselves and send ourselves love. Every time we hear ourselves being self-denigrating, we can change that thought to one of self-appreciation and love.

We can forgive people who have hurt us and forgive others for the mistakes they have made, sending all of them love and compassion instead.

This is how we can have peace in our hearts and, ultimately, in the world.

It feels so freeing to be open and willing to let go of everything that is blocking my heart from love and compassion.

Move into the joy of this moment. That's a sign of inner peace—an unmistakable ability to enjoy each moment.
—John Morton

Take time to stop for a moment. What are you doing right now? Are there people around you? Notice them.

Can you see birds?

Trees?

Grass?

Sky?

When you become aware that you are thinking, just notice that as well.

Smile.

Feel the peace.

Today I am stopping as often as I can throughout the day to feel the peace of the moment.

In the universe there is an immeasurable force which shamans call intent, and absolutely everything that exists in the entire cosmos is attached to intent by a connecting link.
—Carlos Castaneda

Have you ever joined in a rally or a march and felt the energy of everyone believing in the same cause? Or been to a sports event and felt the energy of the crowd as they cheered the home team on to victory? Or been part of a choir or an orchestra where everyone blended together to create beautiful music?

Perhaps you have experienced this energy in other ways, as part of any group with the same intention or purpose. Remember what that felt like then and let yourself feel it again now. Let yourself feel the energy from your connection with millions of people who have world peace as their intention.

Know that we are all connected, that this powerful energy is making it happen. Hold on to this power throughout the day. Know in your heart that peace is happening.

My spirit feels lifted with the knowledge that I am connected to so many people in this world who are creating peace.

Peace is inevitable to those who offer peace.
—*A Course in Miracles*

When we are willing to come together and talk to those
with whom we differ, we can have peace.

When we are willing to really listen to those on the other
side of an argument, we can have peace.

When we don't insist upon our way, when we accept that
there are many views on the same subject, when we
can allow and respect another's point of view, we can
have peace.

When we don't insist upon winning every argument and can
learn to coexist with our differences, we can have peace.

*Today I pray I can let go of my need to win and be right.
I pray I can learn to listen and respect all points of
view with an open mind and a peaceful heart.*

Transforming our difficult emotions and healing the past is a very, very deep practice. For us to be able to transform our own hatred and anger so that we can truly respond in a way that can be skillful and effective runs counter to our conditioning. It is at the heart of all nonviolence.

—Joanne Friday

Acting in a way that is opposite to everything we know and feel is extraordinarily difficult. To be able to let go of the anger and hatred that we feel toward our enemies can feel impossible. It can often take more than time and intention.

It might be that prayer is the only answer to melt our hearts from the bitterness we feel. Alone, we may not have the strength. Praying for this strength to a power greater than ourselves can give us the courage we need to be open to doing what is necessary for peace in our hearts and in the world.

Today I pray for the willingness to let go of my anger and hate so that I might be open to finding a path of peace with my enemies.

Be not angry that you cannot make others as you wish them to be, since you cannot make yourself as you wish to be.
—Thomas à Kempis

A relationship can be a wonderful source of love, support, joy, and peace, or it can be one of stress and unhappiness. When we are not happy we may find ourselves automatically blaming the other person, wishing that he or she would change into the person we want so that we would be happy.

How can we expect someone else to change when, if we are truly honest, we are not the person we wish ourselves to be? Much of the frustration and upset we feel when those near us act in ways we don't like could be eliminated if we were to look at ourselves instead. What can we do to change ourselves? What can we do to increase our own happiness and peace of mind?

Today I am looking within to find my own blocks to peace and happiness. Once I discover them, I will ask God to remove them so that I might be at peace.

Emotion in itself is not unhappiness.
Only emotion plus an unhappy story is.
—Eckhart Tolle

Sad, unpleasant, and disappointing events can and do happen. They are part of life. By staying close to God, knowing where we can turn for comfort and strength, we can get through anything with inner peace, no matter what is going on.

It is when we have a story about our circumstances that we stay stuck in pain and suffering. Our story is our block to inner peace. For example, if the company we are working for closes down and we lose our job, we might say to ourselves and anyone who will listen, "Why does everything happen to me? I have the worst luck. Nothing every goes right in my life." This is our story and we play it over and over and over in our heads, keeping ourselves stuck in misery.

Acceptance is one of the important keys to inner peace. Instead of repeating our story, we can stay with the facts of the situation. "My company closed down. I am out of a job and have to look for a new one." No drama or *poor mes*.

This is not to make light of a difficult or painful situation. It is simply to show that there are many ways of reacting to any situation. Only we have the power to choose what is best for us.

I am practicing acceptance today. I am not magnifying, aggrandizing, or internalizing whatever happens. It feels so good to experience the peace that comes from simply accepting.

The enlightened collective can be a vortex for consciousness
that will accelerate the planetary shift.
—Eckhart Tolle

More and more people around the world are realizing that war only creates more pain, more death, more suffering, more separation, and more differences.

More and more people are saying, "STOP! Let's find another way. Let's come together and find peace."

More and more people are waking up to the realization that our old ways of solving differences have, in the long run, not worked.

I feel the power of our collective consciousness as
I know that together we are spreading peace.

Tolerance is the positive and cordial effort to understand another's beliefs, practices, and habits without necessarily sharing or accepting them.
—Rabbi Joshua Liebman

So many of us are brought up being taught that our race, religion, country, and belief system are the only way, the right way, the best way. We learn to look at others either as wrong or as our enemies.

It takes maturity for us to think for ourselves, reevaluate our early teachings, learn from our own experiences, and, as a result, make our own decisions. As we grow and mature, we can formulate our own new values. As our world expands and we meet new people of all colors and races from all over our planet, we discover that they are, for the most part, very much like us. We all share the same hopes and dreams, fears and concerns. Some might think like us. Others might not.

We learn we can coexist, even with our differences. We can like each other, or at least tolerate each other, even when we don't agree. It is far more peaceful to tolerate our differences than it is to insist that our way is the only way.

I pray I may be open to all people, whether I agree with them or not.

A CHRISTIAN PRAYER FOR PEACE

Steer the ship of my life, good Lord, to your quiet harbor, where I can be safe from the storms of sin and conflict.

Show me the course I should take.

Renew in me the gift of discernment, so that I can always see the right direction in which I should go.

And give me the strength and the courage to choose the right course, even when the sea is rough and the waves are high, knowing that through enduring hardship and danger in your name we shall find comfort and peace.

—Basil of Caesarea

*Mistaking our stories for absolute truth
is the source of alienation.*
—Christina Feldman

If we ever want to make peace with our past, we must let go of our stories.

If we ever want to be open to new experiences, new ways of thinking, new freedom, we must let go of our stories. Our stories are only our perceptions of what we have gone through. As long as we hold on to them, we will be run by them.

We have to let go of all the fears, prejudices, preconceived ideas, and judgments that fill our stories so that we can live each moment with fresh eyes and open hearts.

There is great peace in letting go, just being here, now, in this moment.

As I learn to let go of everything I am holding on to what is keeping me from peace, I am free to see the world as it really is. I am now able to feel peace in each moment.

Progress, not perfection.
—*Alcoholics Anonymous*

Some days peace simply eludes us, no matter how hard we try to find it. No matter how much we know, there can be days when we feel everything but inner peace.

It's okay.

Know that it is okay.

Be as gentle as you can with yourself.

No judgments.

Days like this don't last forever. At any time it could turn around.

Stop when you can to pray and meditate.

Make a gratitude list.

Above all, be compassionate with yourself and know you are doing the best you can, and that is good enough.

No matter how I feel today, I am being gentle with myself.
I know that all moods pass. Nothing is permanent.
I can handle anything one day at a time.

> We would have inward peace, but will not look within.
> —Empedocles

While sitting in my doctor's waiting room one day, I became aware of a ripping sound. I looked up to see the woman sitting across from me tearing pages out of a magazine she held on her lap. She folded each page and then handed it to the woman sitting next to her, who put the pages in her purse.

At first I stared at the woman, hoping she would see that I saw what she was doing, hoping she would realize how wrong she was and stop taking any more pages. As I realized that I was judging her, I remembered a time when I, too, had "stolen" pages from a magazine in a doctor's office. And then I realized I didn't even know if it was the doctor's magazine or her own. Or perhaps she had asked permission to take the pages.

I saw how quick I was to judge and criticize, to feel superior. It felt good to be aware of the change that came over me, from self-righteous indignation to a softening into acceptance. I could feel my tension leaving and my heart opening. I felt peaceful.

Notice how you respond or react internally to what goes on around you today. Be aware, without any judgment, of how you react to things not going your way, to things you think are wrong, to people you view with dislike.

Notice your feelings. Notice your judgments. Let go. Let your heart open. Send love and compassion to yourself and others. Feel the difference. Feel the peace.

Today I am sending love and compassion to everyone I see, regardless of how I feel about them or what they are doing.

315

When I am most at peace, I know that I am living in my heart, that I am held safely in the spirit of the universe and love's sustaining warmth. It is in this special place that I can truly know peace and be grateful.

—Dorna Allen

Home is where the heart is, where many of us live, and where we are most at peace. When we are not living in our hearts, we are often in turmoil. Can the rent be paid? Will it rain to save the dying plants? Who can fix that leaking faucet or that broken door? When will there be a time without a list of things to do? Will the children ever stop fighting? Can we find contentment with our partners? How can we deal with the pain of aging? What can we do about our anger? Are we loved?

A peaceful heart is proof of acceptance of what is and what is not, of dependence on a Higher Power to provide all the strength and support needed to get through one day. A peaceful heart is open to the beauty of nature. A peaceful heart sings the song of belonging.

Peace comes from living in and accepting reality. It comes from within, not from without. It is something to be greatly desired.

Submitted by Dorna L. Allen

I am opening my heart to God, knowing I will receive all the strength and support I need to live in peace.

Look to this day!
For it is life, the very life of Life.

In its brief course lie all the verities and realities of your
    existence.
The bliss of growth, the glory of action, the splendor of beauty;
for yesterday is but a dream, and tomorrow only a vision;
but today well lived makes every yesterday a dream of happiness,
    and every tomorrow a vision of hope.
Look well therefore to this day!
Such is the salutation of the dawn!

—*Kalidasa*

*Peace is not a relationship of nations. It is a condition
of mind brought about by a serenity of soul. Peace is not
merely the absence of war. It is also a state of mind.
Lasting peace can come only to peaceful people.*
—Jawaharlal Nehru

Sometimes thoughts race and tumble in our minds and we find ourselves moving quickly, in circles, racing to keep up with them. We dash about, trying to do too much, trying to be responsible for everything. Even the voices in our minds are saying, "Hurry! Worry!"

We can catch ourselves at those times and talk back to the voices, saying, "Stop. Hurry won't help. Worry accomplishes nothing. Slow down." Then we can think and act with deliberateness, with purpose.

We can take a deep, slow breath, and then another one. Let our shoulders drop, our jaw unclench, our belly and hips relax. Reexamine the long "to do" list and choose the one task that matters most at that moment. Say a little prayer or give someone a hug before he or she leaves for the day. Maybe what we need to do first is not answer the ringing telephone, but close our eyes instead and say a little prayer.

One thing is certain: We can carry Peace with us, like a lighted lamp, sharing it with all with whom we come in contact. Before we can do that, though, we must light the lamp within ourselves and keep it going.

Submitted by Samantha White

---

*It's so freeing to know that whenever I am stressed
I can feel peaceful by stopping, breathing,
and saying to myself, "Peace. Peace. Peace."*

There is no need to go to India or anywhere else to find peace. You will find that deep place of silence right in your room, your garden, or even your bathtub.
—Elisabeth Kübler-Ross

Take time to be quiet each day. Sit in silence.

If your house is big enough, it is wonderful to keep a separate room or a part of a room just for silence, prayer, and meditation. If this isn't possible, your own bed can be your temple. Any place where you can be alone and connect with God is perfect.

If you are not at home, take a break from daily stress and sit in your car.

Stop in a church or a synagogue.

Find a park bench.

There is nothing like time spent in silence to bring us closer to God and help us find peace in our hearts.

Today I am taking time to step out of all activities and take some time for me in silence. Just thinking about this brings me peace.

The most heated bit of letter-writing can be a wonderful safety valve—providing the wastepaper basket is somewhere near by.
—Bill Wilson

Are you angry at someone? Are you holding on to resentment? Is there someone you envy? Someone who has hurt you, taken something from you, or not given you something you want?

Writing a letter to that person is a wonderful release. In the letter we can say everything we would like to say to the person, every feeling we have been holding in. We can write this letter even to someone who has died. If these feelings aren't expressed, they do us harm mentally, physically, and spiritually. It's in expressing them that we find freedom and peace.

Just make sure you wait twenty-four hours before mailing the letter. Give yourself a full twenty-four hours and then reread it. Once your feelings are expressed, you may feel better about the situation and decide either not to send it at all or to write a softer, less angry letter.

I am finding healthy ways to express my feelings today. I no longer keep them bottled up, blocking me from feeling inner peace.

Today
I am sending
healing energy
to
everyone
on the
planet.
May we all
be
healed
and
be
at
peace.

> *Fear is faith in something negative.*
> —*Michael C. Rann and Elizabeth Rann Arrott*

We can get ourselves all worked up predicting how events that have not even occurred will turn out. We fear a plane will crash, a child will get sick, we'll lose our jobs, we'll never have enough money to do the things we want to do in our lives. On and on we think, pessimistically, automatically.

Many of us were taught by example in early childhood to be fearful, and then it became a habit. It's like turning on a radio that gets only one station. We react the same way we learned when we were little.

If any of this sounds like you, know that awareness is the beginning of change. Next time you find yourself predicting doom, stop yourself and let it go. We have only the now. We have no idea how the future will turn out, but we can have faith in a positive outcome. Even if you are uncomfortable with this way of thinking, practice turning your thoughts to faith anyway. You will be amazed to find life changing for the better and the feelings of fear that you have been carrying for so long turning into feelings of peace.

> *I pray that I may let go of my fears today*
> *so that I can have peace in my heart.*

A HOPI LEGEND

When He gathered the peoples of the Earth together on an island that is beneath the waters, He told them, "I am going to send you in the four directions, and over time, I am going to change you into four colors. But I am going to give each of you certain teachings, and when you come back together, you will share these teachings with each other. Then you can live together and have peace upon the Earth, and a great civilization will come about."

*No matter what is going on
in my life today,
I am taking
some time out
to be with nature.
If I can't go outside,
I can look out the window.
If I don't have a window
with a view of nature,
I can go inside myself
and visualize
a beautiful place.
The peace I find in nature
can nurture me
throughout the
rest of my day.*

We all smile in the same language.
—From a poster in an elementary school

Today is a wonderful day to look for the sameness in everyone we meet. What lies beyond our differences of color, race, or religion? What brings us together? What connects us as human beings?

We all bleed when we are cut.

We all smile when we are happy.

We all look at the same moon and stars.

The same sun warms us all.

We have more similarities than differences.

Let's make this a day when we focus on our similarities.

Today I am opening my heart to see our interconnectedness.
I am finding the goodness in everyone.

What do I need to cultivate in this moment to be truly awake?
What do I need to let go of in this moment to be free?
What do I need to learn from this moment to find profound peace?
—Christina Feldman

These are wonderful questions to explore so that we can learn about ourselves. Being fully present in this moment is where we can see our truth, where we can grow, where we find peace.

Look deeply.

Be open.

Have courage

Be truthful.

Today I am taking time to discover how to live with peace
in my heart. The answers are here within me in this
very moment and I am so grateful.

A Muslim Prayer for Peace

In the name of Allah, the beneficent, the merciful. Praise be to the Lord of the Universe who has created us and made us into tribes and nations, that we may know each other, not that we may despise each other. If the enemy incline toward peace, do thou also incline toward peace, and trust in God, for the Lord is the one that heareth and knoweth all things. And the servants of God, Most Gracious, are those who walk on the Earth in humility, and when we address them, we say "Peace."

*There came a time when the risk to remain tight in the bud
was more painful than the risk it took to blossom.*

—Anaïs Nin

Change, as we well know, is very difficult. We get into habits and routines and they are often hard to break. Many years ago, addiction expert Father Joseph C. Martin made a film of one of his lectures, called "Chalk Talks," in which he explained how hard it is to change a habit. He suggested that if you wear your watch on your right wrist, change it to the left wrist and see how long you keep glancing at your right wrist for the time.

Please don't get discouraged with the changes you are trying to make in your life. If you have become aware of any negative or judgmental patterns in your thinking, you have probably had these patterns for many years. Turning your negative thoughts around to positive thoughts and your judgmental thoughts to thoughts of acceptance will take time and attention. Maxwell Maltz, in his book *Psycho-Cybernetics*, wrote about his observations and experiments as a surgeon. Dr. Maltz observed that after plastic surgery it took patients twenty-one days to see their improved condition and think they looked better. He followed this up with other experiments that proved this same point, concluding that it takes twenty-one days to make a change.

So be gentle with yourself. You will be pleased to see how much more peaceful you will feel as the new patterns become more and more a natural part of your thinking.

*I pray that I have the patience and intention needed to
change into the more peaceful person I want to be.*

I send my love out into the universe, attracting all the people,
places, and things that best benefit me. I send my love out into
the universe, attracting all the people, places, and things that
I can best benefit, and I say COME NOW.

—Author unknown

A friend taught me this prayer many years ago, and over the years I have gone through periods where I say it often in the morning after my other prayers and my meditation. I have found that it opens me up to a wonderful energy and to a spiritual connection with the people I meet during the day. While I might have met them without this prayer, when I say it I am aware that I more often find myself in the presence of people who can help me or whom I can help.

My friend suggested that I *shout* this prayer in the morning, and I do shout it sometimes. More often I say it quietly to myself and open myself up to the mysteries of the day.

Today I am open to everyone who comes into my life.
It's a wonderful feeling to know there are people in this
world who can help me and people whom I can help.

You have heard that it was said, "You shall love your neighbor and hate your enemy." But I say to you, love your enemies, bless those who curse you, do good to those who hate you, and pray for those who spitefully use you and persecute you.
—Matthew 5:43-44

Many wise and spiritual teachers and saints suggest that we pray for our enemies. This is, at first, a very difficult thing to do, and we may resist even the thought of this suggestion. More often, when we think of our enemies, we feel anger, fear, or resentment. Our hearts close and we want to strike back, punish them, or get even after all they have done to us or to our country or to those we love.

Let's look at this in a different way. Think for a moment about how you feel when you are angry and want revenge. Are your fists clenched? Is your jaw tight? Do you feel churning in your stomach? Now look at how you feel when you think of a person for whom you have love and compassion. See how your body relaxes. See how much more peaceful you feel.

In this light we can see that we do want our enemies' hearts to soften. If their hearts and ours were full of love and compassion, war, murder, and crime could become obsolete.

I pray that everyone on earth be filled with love and compassion, that all wars and violence cease, and that we all live in peace.

True peace is not a destination into the future
but a path and practice of the moment.
—Christina Feldman

Where am I right now?

What am I thinking?

What am I craving?

What do I like?

What don't I like?

Who am I in this moment?

How am I feeling?

Do I like myself?

Am I satisfied with myself?

Do I have enough?

Am I enough?

These are some questions you can ask yourself in any given moment. What is keeping you from saying YES to the last four questions? Self-awareness is discovering your blocks to inner peace and seeing how your own cravings, opinions, aversions, judgments, and desires decide for you whether or not you are at peace.

It doesn't really matter what is going on outside us; it's what is going on inside us that can make each moment one of peace.

Today I am looking deeply into my own nature and praying
that I let go of all my blocks to inner peace.

*In the silence, I touch the presence of God
within and find perfect peace.*
—from Daily Word magazine

My quest for peace began as far back as I can remember. I was to seek peace externally for many years through books, music, religion, emotional and financial security, people, and finally alcohol. And always it eluded me. Following many years of pain and struggle, Grace gently guided me through life challenges that were to serve as transformational opportunities. I was to discover that forgiveness is the pathway to peace. I was to discover that Love is synonymous with God, and "the peace of God which surpasses all understanding" is always available to me.

Submitted by Barbara Thomas

*I ask in my daily prayers for peace in my family,
peace in my country, and peace in the world. My daily
conscious contact with God nurtures inner peace.*

Being aware of your breath forces you into the present moment—the key to inner transformation.
—Eckhart Tolle

Take three mindful breaths as often as you can during the day. Notice the space between your breaths, the gap between the in breath and the out breath. In this space you can feel extraordinary peace. It can expand your energy.

Take three mindful breaths as often as you can during the day, especially during conversations. It can help you be present and, therefore, be a better listener.

Take three mindful breaths as often as you can during the day, especially when you are angry, fearful, upset, stressed, or disappointed.

Take three mindful breaths as often as you can during the day, especially when you want to act on an unhealthy thought. It helps you to stop when you feel a compulsion to do something you are trying not to do, such as drinking or taking drugs or eating that piece of chocolate cake.

Take three mindful breaths as often as you can during the day and feel the peace.

I am practicing mindful breathing each day and my life is becoming more and more peaceful. I am so grateful.

Who am I when no one is looking?
—Author unknown

Think about the stress that you feel when you are out to impress someone. Perhaps you are going for a job interview or simply trying to get in with a group. You might feel tension in your body. Your breath might be shallow. Your mind is probably racing, trying to think of the right words to say so that the person you are pretending to be will be accepted.

Now imagine how you feel when you are just you—no acting—no pressure—just yourself. You can feel your entire body relaxing. You might even notice that you are smiling. Your breath is more natural and you are certainly not clenching your jaw or your fists.

The choice is yours. How would you like to feel today?

I pray for the confidence to present myself exactly as I am and to love myself for who I am.

The less you carry, the farther you go. So let go!
—Chuck Gallozzi

There is a Buddhist lesson that clearly explains how we create our own suffering by holding on. If an arrow enters your body, it hurts. If another arrow enters the same spot, it hurts tenfold.

When someone insults us, or is angry with us, or treats us in a way that is disrespectful, it hurts us. This is the first arrow. When we cannot let it go, when we go over and over it in our minds, that is the second arrow. The pain is magnified, and this time we are doing it to ourselves.

Today I pray that I can let go of all that I am holding on to that is causing me suffering and blocking me from peace.

What will you do with your one wild and precious life?
—Mary Oliver

We can go through our lives putting the greatest emphasis on ourselves and placing money, material goods, success, and fame first—

or

we can focus on finding ways we can help others and be a beacon for peace in the world.

The choice is ours.

I am putting aside some time to examine where I am in my life today. What is most important to me now and what are my goals for the future? I pray for the knowledge of God's will for me and the power to carry it out.

I feel
connected
with everyone
reading
this page
today.
I feel our
oneness,
our love,
our compassion,
our peace.
I feel
our power
as we send
peace
out
into
the
world.

How Can I Help?
—Title of a book by Ram Dass and Paul Gorman

This is a wonderful prayer to say first thing in the morning and to remember during the day. This doesn't mean that we neglect ourselves to help others. If we are in need, we can't be of service to others. Therefore we may ask the question, "How can I help?" of ourselves for our own self-care.

And once we have taken care of ourselves, this question then helps us get out of our own self-centeredness and expand our vision of what this day can be. It helps us stretch our hearts open with the willingness to go beyond our own needs and do something for someone else.

May my eyes and ears and heart stay open to the cries of the world today. May I have the strength and the willingness to help bring peace to others whenever and wherever I can.

*Practicing the Immeasurable Mind of Compassion extinguishes
all sorrows and anxieties in the heart of living beings.*
—Nagarjuna

Enough cannot be said about compassion as a gateway to inner and outer peace. Just as peace begins in our own hearts before we can send it out into the world, compassion works the same way. We learn to have compassion for ourselves before we can have compassion for anyone else. We do this by stopping the judgments we have about ourselves. We can do this by listening to how we speak to ourselves and stopping our thoughts when we put ourselves down, compare ourselves to others, and say we are not being good enough.

We can feel our fears and regrets. We can look at and accept our imperfections. Perhaps we are clumsy or tone-deaf. Perhaps we can't hit a baseball or we limp. Maybe we have a poor memory or no sense of direction. Whatever our imperfections may be, we can look at ourselves with the eyes of love and compassion. These qualities grow out of acceptance.

Only in letting go of our judgments about ourselves and accepting ourselves can we find peace. Not until we can release our own suffering can we have compassion for anyone else.

*Today I am looking for opportunities to soften my heart
by giving myself love and compassion. I deserve to be happy.
I deserve to be peaceful. Compassion can bring me these gifts.*

God speaks: From the highest mountain it has been shouted,
in the lowest places its whisper has been heard.
Through the corridors of all human experience has this Truth
been echoed: Love is the answer. Yet you have not listened.
—Neale Donald Walsch

Century after century, by philosophers, poets, saints, sages, and religious and spiritual leaders, the power of love has been taught.

Let's listen today.

Today I am listening, seeing, acting, and thinking
from an open and loving heart. I am at peace.

I have been through some terrible things in my life,
some of which actually happened.
—Mark Twain

Fear is a healthy instinct that can save our lives, but most of the time fear originates in our minds in the form of something that hasn't occurred. These imagined fears cause us stress and unnecessary suffering. They usually stem from the thought of losing something we already have or not getting something we want. Fear can keep us up at night, ruin our appetites, block our memories, and cause life-threatening physical and mental illnesses. Fear comes only when we live in the future and not in the present moment.

Faith is the other side of fear. Turning our fears over to a power greater than ourselves is the perfect key to inner peace. In fact, turning everything over to God, living with the faith that God is in charge, can bring us peace and joy beyond our wildest imagination.

I am flooded with peace today as I turn
all my fears over to the care of God.

Nothing is so fatiguing as the eternal
hanging on of an uncompleted task.
—William James

Procrastination is one of the greatest enemies of inner peace. Often driven by fear of failure, we put off large and small tasks to the last minute, building more and more tension as the deadline gets closer and closer. We can create endless excuses when we are late and make sincere vows that we will do better in the future.

Sometimes mere laziness, not fear, is our motive. At other times it might be poor time management, putting other, less important things first, or simply hoping the task will disappear.

Procrastination can be a subtle addiction. For example, say you have something due in two weeks. As the first week goes by, your tension builds. Every day the pressure mounts and mounts until finally, on the fourteenth day, you finish your task and get it in on time. The pressure is off. What a relief! You feel ecstatic! It gives you a natural high, which can be a subconscious motivator to procrastinate another time.

Doing something early or on time does not have the same ecstatic payoff, nor does it create the same tension. It is quiet. It is peaceful. It is freeing.

It feels so peaceful to do everything on time today.

When despair for the world grows in me,
and I wake in the night at the least sound
in fear of what my life and my children's lives may be—
I go and lie down where the wood drake rests in his beauty
on the water and the great heron feeds. I come into the
peace of wild things who do not tax their lives with forethought
or grief. I come into the presence of still water. And I feel
above me the day-blind stars waiting with their light.
For a time I rest in the grace of the world, and am free.
—Wendell Berry

Grace is that which happens to us when we are not looking for it. Grace is the pause between sentences when we decide to get honest. Grace is actually God's gift to mankind. It connects us and binds us together, the silent whisper of connection to every living thing.

Submitted by Heather Lowe

I trust that God's grace is with all of us today
and the world is filled with peace.

*When two great forces oppose each other, the victory
will go to the one that knows how to yield.*
—Tao Te Ching

We can choose to wade through the waters of life attempting to control our circumstances, we can fight with every rock that appears in our path, or we can choose to let go and flow with the current, drifting around the rocks, all the while savoring the ride.

Peace is a choice to yield to the universe. As we trust that the river will take us exactly where we need to go, the riverbanks transform from an unfriendly place to a world teeming with abundance, with unlimited possibility and sustenance. Peace surfaces as we choose to flow with life no matter what obstacles line the path. True peace arises with accepting life just as it is.

Submitted by Janet Glass

I trust the river and go with the flow of life today.

*To enter the silent world of peace requires
that we learn the secret of being still. We must discover
and enter into our own still being.*
—Guy Finley

We often have a vision of where we would find peace, a specific place where, if we go there, all will be fine. For some it's lying on a blanket with a cloudless sky overhead, listening to the gentle sound of the waves moving in and out. For others it's hiking up a mountain to the very top and looking over the world, or just cocooning in a favorite chair and being alone.

These places are just catalysts. Peace is deep within us. It's acceptance. It's grounding. It's the breath flowing in and out, acknowledging the moment for what it is.

Submitted by Sandy Martin

*I am stopping all my activity now and being still.
I feel my breath going in and going out.
I feel full of peace.*

I can feel the
power of our
thoughts
as I join
with
others
and we
send
our energy
for peace
out
into
the world.

Faith is the bird that sings when the dawn is still dark.
—Rabindranath Tagore

There are days when answers just aren't there, when we really just don't know what to do about certain situations in our lives. There are days when we feel alone, abandoned by God; when inner peace seems as if it is not meant for us.

There are times when we are in a mood so black that we fear never seeing the light again.

These are the times to hang in there. No mood is permanent, and whether you believe it or not, this too shall pass. These are the times for blind faith, for praying even if you doubt the existence of a power greater than yourself. Simply going through the motions of praying, acting as if you believe, can often help you get to the opposite side of doubt.

It can help to look at a plant, flower, or tree. Watch a sunrise or a sunset. Know that there is a life force beyond yourself whether you can feel it or not.

I pray that I can feel connected to a power greater than myself and feel peace with this connection.

A Buddhist Prayer for Peace

May all beings everywhere plagued with sufferings of body and mind quickly be freed from their illnesses. May those frightened cease to be afraid, and may those bound be free. May the powerless find power, and may people think of befriending one another. May those who find themselves in trackless, fearful wildernesses—the children, the aged, the unprotected—be guarded by beneficent celestials, and may they swiftly attain Buddhahood.

Today I am being
mindful of my breath.
Every time I
breathe in
I know
the loving
energy of
peace
flows into
my heart.
As I breathe out,
this energy flows
out
of
my
heart
and travels
to the
hearts
of
everyone
around the
world.

Every time you smile at someone, it is an action of love,
a gift to that person, a beautiful thing.
—*Mother Teresa*

When I was much younger, I was so shy that when I passed people on the sidewalk I would look down, not daring eye contact. Grateful that that has all changed for me now, I actually enjoy smiling at people I pass, sometimes nodding my head in greeting and sometimes even saying hello. A dear friend enjoys sending loving thoughts to people she passes in the supermarket, knowing she's spreading love to all those people.

Why not make today a peace day for you? Wherever you are, send loving and peaceful energy to anyone you see. Think of your friends and family, whether you are with them or not, and send them peace and love. Then think of other people you know and send *them* thoughts of peace and love. And then, if you really want some freedom and peace in your own life, send thoughts of peace and love to anyone with whom you are having any difficulty or whom you just don't like. And then send thoughts of peace and love to everyone in the world.

Smiling at strangers and sending out thoughts of peace
and love fills me with great joy. It expands my heart
and makes me feel close to all human beings.

The best way to find yourself is to lose yourself
in the service of others.
—Mahatma Gandhi

Whom can I help today?

What can I do to participate in making our world more peaceful?

Please help me to stay awake and alert to
opportunities of service today, God, and to take
an action step when You show me one.

He who angers you conquers you.
—Elizabeth Kenny

Although it might be hard to understand at times, when we are angry at someone, they have not "made" us angry. Anger was already in us; what happened outside of us triggered our internal anger. The same is true for jealousy, resentment, fear, and all of our other emotions. We really have all emotions at some level within us. Some are more easily triggered than others.

Once we know we are responsible for our feelings and accept them as they come up, it is easier to let them go. Breathing in and out three times helps us withhold an angry response to someone who has triggered our own anger. Breathing in and out three times keeps us from lashing out to hurt the person who has hurt us.

It is very freeing to look deeply into ourselves and find the source of all these feelings that create so much pain and suffering. We can then pray for healing and peace.

I pray for restraint of tongue and pen. I pray that I may express only positive and loving feelings today.

*Nobody made a greater mistake than he who did
nothing because he could only do a little.*
—Edmund Burke

There is a wonderful story about two women who were walking along the beach. They saw hundreds of starfish, which had been left on the shore from a recent storm. One woman began throwing the starfish back into the sea.

"Why are you doing that? You can't save all those starfish," said the other woman.

"But I can save this one. And this one. And this one."

So it is with us. We can help, one person at a time.

*Today I am doing whatever I can to make at
least one person's life a little brighter.*

Prayer draws us near to our own souls.
—Herman Melville

The most important thing I have to do today is to connect with my Higher Power, whatever I call this power greater than myself. The name may be God, Allah, Spirit, Universal Energy, Goddess, or something else. Someone once suggested that I put the letter *o* in the middle of the word *God* and pray to the power of good. He pointed out that God can be the power of love as well. These suggestions helped me until I was able to be comfortable with the God of my understanding, my own interpretation of God.

When we make this spiritual connection the first thing in our day, our entire day goes more smoothly. We know we are on a spiritual path. We can feel this power with us throughout the day. We can turn to this power and ask for guidance for whatever is happening in our day. We are never alone.

I can feel peace in my heart when I connect with the God of my understanding. I am so grateful.

As each of you realize your own worth and value, you will add, one by one, to the consciousness of unlimited thinking, unlimited freedom, and unlimited love. Whatever you think, whatever you come to realize, lifts and expands consciousness everywhere.
—Ramtha

As more and more of us experience the power of our thoughts, we see how we have the power to make a difference in the world. It is important that we teach other people what we know. Let us help people to understand that our thoughts are energy and that others can feel this energy.

As more and more of us awaken to this knowledge, we are lifting the consciousness of the world to a new level of understanding, to peace.

It is exciting to share with other people what I am learning and practicing in my own life. Together we are bringing peace to our planet.

It brings me
great joy
to know
we are all
interconnected
on our
special path
toward
peace.

The greatest discovery of all time is that a person can change his future by merely changing his attitude.
—Oprah Winfrey

To create world peace, the first steps are self-reflection and self-understanding. These steps lead us to a sense of responsibility for our actions. To the extent that we heal ourselves (by knowing who we are and accepting ourselves), we can be open and accepting of others. It is this self-healing that creates the society where, undefended, we freely and safely express ourselves and live the life we most deeply desire.

Submitted by Hannah Reich

Today I am finding different ways to remind myself of peace. The more awareness I bring to this pursuit, the more peaceful I am.

A Jainist Prayer for Peace

Peace and Universal Love are the essence of the Gospel preached by all the Enlightened Ones. The Lord has preached that equanimity is the Dharma. Forgive do I creatures all, and let all creatures forgive me. Unto all have I amity, and unto none enmity. Know that violence is the root cause of all miseries in the world. Violence, in fact, is the knot of bondage. "Do not injure any living being." This is the eternal, perennial, and unalterable way of spiritual life. A weapon, howsoever powerful it may be, can always be superseded by a superior one; but no weapon can, however, be superior to nonviolence and love.

*You cannot add to the peace and goodwill of the
world if you fail to create an atmosphere of harmony
and love right where you live and work.*
—Thomas Dreier

As I find myself concerned with peace around me, I feel it necessary to find it inside myself first. I find it in quiet moments of meditation when I take myself to my safe place, the beach. I feel the sun on my skin, the waves rolling in and out.

If everyone would take a short period of time every day to go inside to their own quiet places, we would all have at least a few moments of peace in our lives. Others will be touched by it as we pass it on.

Submitted by Debbie Boisseau

*I am spending a few quiet moments with myself today and
making a difference in the world. It is so powerful to know that
as I feel peace, my energy expands to everyone around me.*

Peace is not simply the absence of violence;
it is the cultivation of understanding, insight,
and compassion, combined with action.
—Thich Nhat Hanh

Peace is a practice. Peace is what we practice right here, right now, in this moment. Most of us have to learn how to have peace. We have to be mindful of what brings us peace and what takes away our peace. We have to notice the results of our thoughts and our actions.

As you go about your day, be mindful of how you feel in different situations. Examine how you feel when watching a violent movie or television program. What happens inside of you when you give in to an addiction or indulge in other unhealthy habits? What is the emotional result of letting your mind wander into fantasies of revenge? Note the difference in how you feel when you meditate and when you forget to meditate.

In order to have inner peace right now, right here, we have to develop new habits and let go of old ones. We have to be a witness to ourselves and learn and change.

Today I am paying very close attention to my thoughts
and my actions so that I can learn what I need to change
in order to have peace in my heart.

*In the attitude of silence the soul finds the path in a clearer light,
and what is elusive and deceptive resolves itself into crystal
clearness. Our life is a long and arduous quest after Truth.*
—Mahatma Gandhi

One of the most peaceful things we can do for ourselves is to give ourselves the gift of a silent, mindful meal. If you cannot do this today, save the idea for another time.

Turn off your radio, television, MP3 player, cell phone, and landline phone. Some people go a step further and, for a short time, turn off any appliances that make noise. Put aside books, newspapers, and other reading material.

Just be with the experience of eating. Be aware of the taste and the texture of the food. Chew slowly. Be mindful of your thoughts and your emotions. Be with whatever comes up for you and accept it without judgment. For example, if you feel impatient and want to stop the silence, notice what that feels like and stay with it. Learn from your impatience. See what impatience feels like in your mind and your body. If you are peaceful, notice what this feels like and enjoy.

Simply be. Taste. Smell. Touch. Feel. Hear. Be mindful of the entire experience.

Perhaps you might want to spend one silent meal a day or one a week. Perhaps not. It might take a few times to get used to it. Give it a try. This is a wonderful way to practice peace.

*By spending time away from all the noise that fills my day,
I find deep peace in the silence.*

When we see God in each other, then we will have peace.
—*Mother Teresa*

When we see each other as equals, all deserving to have food on the table, a safe place to live, and clothes on our backs, then we shall have peace and harmony. One way to achieve this is to begin to believe that there is "enough" for everyone. That there is enough for everyone is difficult to envision, yet there is abundance in the world.

By recognizing that each of us has something to share, whether it be talents, money, blessings, food, water, housing, or love, we begin to "see God in each other" that Mother Teresa speaks of. When we believe that everyone has the right to share in this abundance, it becomes easier to access the common good in one another and to become equals. We will have no reason to fight, bicker, or go to war with one another. We can work together in harmony and join each other in the family of one world and peace.

Submitted by Deborah Ann Hagen

I pray that I may be generous and willing to share, so that we will all have enough.

First they came for the Jews. I was silent. I was not a Jew.
Then they came for the Communists. I was silent.
I was not a Communist. Then they came for the trade unionists.
I was silent. I was not a trade unionist.
Then they came for me. There was no one left to speak for me.
—Martin Niemöller

I will not be silent when someone needs help.

God, please give me courage and guidance
to support the freedom and safety of all human beings
wherever and whenever possible.

Seeds, like hearts, must open to grow.
—Carol Horos

Imagine your heart is an empty container, shaped like a
   valentine, and there is a large opening at the top.
Now imagine that God is pouring love into this opening.
And now compassion.
And now generosity.
And now equanimity.
And now peace.
Feel each word as you say it to yourself, as you imagine it
   pouring it into your heart.
Know that you have all these qualities in you. They are
   always here for you.
All you have to do is turn to your heart and feel them.

I am so grateful for my God-given gifts.

I believe that uncertainty is really my spirit's way
of whispering, "I'm in flux. I can't decide for you.
Something is off-balance here."
—Oprah Winfrey

A great barrier to inner peace is indecision. Should I? Shouldn't I? Will I? Won't I? We can get so caught up when we don't know what to do about a situation that we may miss great opportunities while we drive ourselves crazy with the stress of going back and forth.

Many years ago, a wise man suggested to me that you can make any decision just for today. Almost any decision can be changed tomorrow. Simply by deciding *yes, no,* or *I don't know,* we can come to a place of peace for this day. Bringing a decision down to one of these three choices can take the stress out of our struggle.

Praying and meditating can help, as can talking to friends and advisors. Gathering pertinent information is also valuable in making an intelligent decision. Then decide *yes, no,* or *I don't know.* In the place of not knowing, where there is often tension, simply let go. In that quiet space, wait for answers to surface.

Today I am doing all I can to resolve any decisions
I have to make. Then I will rest in the peace of knowing
that I will have my answer when the time is right.

Let
there
be
peace
on
earth
and
let
it
begin
with
me.

Index

215, 236, 241, 249, 294, 298, 300,
329, 336, 338, 351, 353, 363
Higher Power (greater power), 24,
32, 44, 50, 61, 90, 107, 112, 128, 136,
139, 171, 247, 256, 257, 262, 269, 272,
273, 287, 297, 302, 307, 316, 347, 354.
See also God
History, 57, 60, 117, 216, 244, 291
Honesty, 147, 176, 239, 253
Hope, 79, 198, 212, 254, 317
Hopelessness, 55, 60, 66, 184, 252
Hopi legend, 323
Humility, 120, 194, 327

I

Impatience, 82, 174, 185, 198, 361
Inspiration, 23, 43, 105, 136, 137, 149,
155, 188, 260
Intention, 16, 24, 42, 101, 106, 142,
151, 188, 257, 260, 269, 305, 307
Intuition, 236, 246

J

Joy, 4, 11, 13, 31, 52, 66, 68, 78, 86, 88,
95, 122, 130, 136, 137, 138, 144, 149,
157, 164, 187, 194, 201, 202, 227, 233,
244, 254, 264, 286, 288, 294, 300,
304, 341, 350, 356
Judgments, 5, 9, 24, 31, 36, 42, 72, 87,
88, 108, 120, 143, 162, 185, 195, 205,
208, 215, 221, 228, 234, 284, 313,
314, 315, 328, 331, 339, 361

K

Kindness, 4, 20, 41, 48, 211, 229, 239

L

Letting go, 16, 29, 30, 33, 36, 51, 54, 55,
62, 72, 97, 98, 107, 108, 123, 125,
128, 133, 136, 140, 144, 151, 152, 160,
171, 175, 176, 189, 195, 196, 208, 216,

219, 227, 242, 248, 249, 256, 257,
263, 266, 277, 284, 285, 287, 293,
295, 303, 306, 307, 313, 315, 322, 326,
331, 335, 339, 344, 360, 365
Light, 75, 76, 91, 150, 175, 177, 178,
189, 194, 225, 254, 281, 283, 318
Listening, 6, 12, 118, 145, 148, 168,
196, 213, 236, 241, 246, 249, 263,
306, 333, 340
Loss, 32, 125, 276, 341. *See also* Pain
and suffering
Love
acceptance and. *See* Acceptance
blocks to, 33, 37, 51, 61, 86, 93, 171.
See also Habits; Negative
thoughts and emotions; Patterns
changing thoughts to, 195
choosing, 3, 80, 144, 162, 195, 238, 252
compassion and. *See* Compassion
cultivating/expanding, 127, 140,
155, 157, 162, 173, 219, 256, 257,
264, 270, 315, 329, 349, 350, 364
desire for, 100
effects of, 270, 283
endurance of, 60
for enemies, 226, 330
fear and. *See* Fear
for fellow humans, 141
fruit of, 27
God as, 332
God's plan for, 252
heart as seat of, 67, 96, 145, 155,
157
joy as, 52. *See also* Joy
loss of, 32
of/for children, 211, 229
of/for self, 152, 172, 303, 315, 339
openness to. *See* Letting go;
Openness
power of, 85, 207, 209, 340, 354

Books and CDs by Ruth Fishel

BOOKS

Living Light as a Feather

Change Almost Anything in 21 Days

Hang In 'Til the Miracle Happens

Precious Solitude

Stop! Do You Know You're Breathing? Simple Techniques for Teachers and Parents to Reduce Stress and Violence in the Classroom and at Home

The Journey Within: A Spiritual Path to Recovery

Time for Joy, Daily Meditations and Affirmations (over 300,000 copies sold)

Time for Thoughtfulness

Take Time for Yourself!

Cape Cod Memories

Newport Memories

Memories of the Florida Coast

CDs

You Can't Meditate Wrong

The Power of Loving Kindness

About the Author

Ruth Fishel, M Ed, is cofounder of Spirithaven of Cape Cod and Florida, which offers retreats, workshops, classes, CDs, and a spiritual and inspirational line of greeting cards. Her books include the best-selling *Living Light as a Feather, Change Almost Anything in 21 Days, Time for Joy, The Journey Within, Hang In 'Til the Miracle Happens, Stop! Do You Know You're Breathing?,* and *Precious Solitude.*

Ruth has also created Spiritlifters, a line of inspirational greeting cards. Her classes, books, and workshops take you on a marvelous journey through pain and loss to inspiration and hope. They provide you with a gentle path to growth, peace, and love.

For more information, go to www.spirithaven.com and peaceinourhearts.net. Call 508-776-3815 or send an e-mail to spirithaven@spirithaven.com for Ruth's workshop schedule or to schedule a talk or workshop.